the Language of Song

Selected and edited by
Nicola-Jane Kemp and Heidi Pegler

FABER *ff* MUSIC

CONTENTS

HOW TO USE THIS BOOK

The Language of Song series was devised especially for the student singer as an introduction to a wealth of classical song repertoire, and to give them the tools and confidence required to sing in the primary mainland European languages. For this reason, no sung English translations are provided. The songs have been carefully chosen for their appropriateness of text and vocal range for the young student singer.

Preface to each song

Each song or aria is prefaced by a page of notes, containing: a brief background (setting it in its historical context or, where appropriate, its place in the drama); an idiomatic translation; and a phonetic pronunciation of the text. Any further notes at the bottom of each page highlight particular language points that may arise in the individual texts.

Translations: There are two translations for each song or aria. The first is a word-for-word translation directly underneath the text in the musical score. This is to enable the student to see exactly which words will be important for emphasis and interpretation. In addition, the prefatory page to each song includes an idiomatic translation, which will clarify the meaning of the text in grammatical English.

Phonetic pronunciation: A phonetic pronunciation of the original language, using the International Phonetic Alphabet (IPA), is provided for each song. A key to pronunciation is provided for each language at the back of this book and includes both examples from the song texts together with the closest English equivalents to the sounds explained. IPA symbols are given in these guides and careful study of these pages will be required in order to fully understand the IPA symbols that accompany the text for each song or aria. These are some of the basic principles that will help the singer to work along the right lines until they are able to refine pronunciation further with the help of a specialist language coach.

The accompanying CDs

The CDs provide the text for each song or aria spoken by the language consultants, all of whom are native speakers and work regularly with professional singers (see Biographies below). The speakers have attempted to make the text as clear as possible whilst maintaining the overall flow and dramatic content of the language. It is recommended that the language texts are prepared independently from the musical melody at first, as follows:

- Read the pronunciation key for the relevant language.
- Listen to the text on the CD, following the IPA guide for the song.
- Practise speaking the text slowly and clearly.
- When confident, slowly speak the text in the rhythm of the music.
- Gradually increase your speed to match the speed of the song.
- Additionally, practise delivering the text as a dramatic recitation showing your understanding of the language.

The CDs also include backing accompaniments for each song or aria. It should be remembered that these are a practice aid only and should not be substituted for a live accompaniment in performance.

Wherever possible, every effort has been made to return to the original source material. New accompaniments have been arranged for the Arie Antique and some (optional) ornamentation suggested, which appears in small staff notation above the vocal line. Editorial additions, such as dynamics, appear in square brackets.

EDITORS & CONSULTANTS: BIOGRAPHIES

Nicola-Jane Kemp

Nicola-Jane is a professional singer, specialising in the coloratura repertoire (her signature role is 'Queen of the Night'), and works for companies as diverse as Music Theatre Wales and the Festival Lyrique d'Aix-en-Provence, France. She has been broadcast on BBC Radio and her concert work takes her all over the UK – including the South Bank, the Barbican, St Martin-in-the-Fields and St John's, Smith Square in London – and to the Middle East. She is an examiner for the Associated Board of the Royal Schools of Music and currently teaches voice to choral scholars at Clare and Queens' Colleges in Cambridge, and at St Paul's Girls' School, Hammersmith, London.

Heidi Pegler

Heidi is Head of Singing at St Paul's Girls' School in London, where she runs a lively and busy singing department. She is an examiner for the Associated Board of the Royal Schools of Music. She was a contributor to both *A Common Approach 2002* and *All Together!* – a book focusing on teaching music in groups (ABRSM). As a professional singer, she specialises in Baroque music (her debut solo CD, *Hark! the echoing air*, features Baroque music for Soprano, Trumpet and Orchestra) and has performed at many of Britain's leading venues including the Royal Albert Hall in London, St David's Hall, Cardiff and the Royal Concert Hall, Glasgow.

Tina Ruta (Italian Consultant)

Born in Naples, Tina studied there at the Conservatoire San Pietro a Maiella and continued her studies with Mark Raphael and Herbert-Caesari in England. As a singer, she has performed in operas and recitals in England, France and Italy and has appeared in London's West End, at Glyndebourne, and in television plays. She has since gone on to develop a highly sought-after practice as an Italian language coach and has taught at the Guildhall School of Music and Drama and Trinity College of Music, both of which awarded her fellowships. She has also coached singers at Covent Garden, Le Châtelet, Opera-Bastille, La Monnaie, Brussels, Berlin State Opera, Vienna State Opera and Volksoper, Bavarian State Opera, Helsinki Opera House, the Sibelius and Amsterdam conservatoires, and for record labels Phillips, Decca, Deutsche Grammophon and EMI. In the course of her work, Tina has collaborated with many conductors, including Giulini, Muti, Sinopoli, Colin Davis, Myung Whun Chung and Pappano. She also translates film scripts, librettos and lyrics.

Franziska Roth (German Consultant)

Franziska was born and grew up in Germany. She studied musicology at Salzburg University, and continued her studies in piano and singing at the 'Mozarteum' Academy of Music. She has worked as a language coach for opera productions at Covent Garden, Glyndebourne, Le Châtelet and Opera-Bastille in Paris; festivals in Aix-en-Provence and Salzburg, and for staged projects in Carnegie Hall, New York. She is highly sought after by many of the world's leading singers as a Lieder and oratorio coach, and has worked for many great conductors, including Barenboim, Rattle, Solti, Haitink, Ghergiev, Pappano, Gardiner and Thielemann. She is also regularly employed by the major recording companies, including EMI, Deutsche Grammophon, Decca, Sony and Chandos. She has been a member of the teaching staff at the Royal College of Music, London since 1989.

Michel Vallat (French Consultant)

Michel Vallat was born in France. He studied at the Sorbonne in Paris, where he graduated with a degree in Philosophy, and at the Conservatoire National Superieur de Musique de Paris, where he won both the *Premier Prix de chant* and the *Premier Prix d'Art lyrique*. Michel undertook further studies in French mélodie with Gerard Souzay, and also studied in Italy with Maestro Valdomiro Badiali and Carlo Bergonzi. He was later appointed French coach at the Royal College of Music and Professor of Singing at the Guildhall School of Music and Drama, London. He works regularly with Welsh National Opera, Scottish Opera, the Glyndebourne Festival and the Royal Opera House (Covent Garden), and with singers such as Valerie Masterson, Della Jones, Thomas Hampson, Sergiev Leeferkus, Bruce Ford, Renée Fleming, David Daniels, Sally Matthews, Joseph Calleja, Angelika Kirchschlager and Christopher Maltman.

Ludmilla Andrew (Russian Consultant)

Ludmilla was born in Canada of Russian parentage and has enjoyed a distinguished international career with the world's leading operas companies, including San Francisco Opera and New York's Metropolitan Opera. She has sung many of the great dramatic soprano title roles, including *Madame Butterfly*, *Tosca*, *Turandot*, *Aida*, *Lady Macbeth*, *Anna Bolena* and *Norma*. She has also specialised in Russian repertoire, with a recital of Russian songs by Nicolai Medtner included amongst her many recordings. She is now one of Britain's leading vocal coaches, working with many young singers, and is frequently invited to sit on competition and opera casting panels. She is the Russian coach at the Royal Academy of Music, London and also vocal and language coach for Chandos Records.

The Editors wish to thank the following for their invaluable contribution to the production of this book: Richard Shaw for advice on Russian; Coral Johnson for Italian manuscripts; Nigel Foster for repertoire advice and general assistance; and St Paul's Girls' School for the generous use of its premises during the CD recording.

© 2008 by Faber Music Ltd
This corrected edition first published in 2013
Bloomsbury House 74–77 Great Russell Street London WC1B 3DA
Cover design by Økvik Design
Music processed by MusicSet 2000
Additional processing by Ashley Harries
Printed in England by Caligraving Ltd
All rights reserved

ISBN10: 0-571-53077-X
EAN13: 978-0-571-53077-9

To buy Faber Music publications or to find out about the full range of titles available
please contact your local music retailer or Faber Music sales enquiries:

Faber Music Limited, Burnt Mill, Elizabeth Way, Harlow, CM20 2HX England
Tel: +44 (0)1279 82 89 82   Fax: +44 (0)1279 82 89 83
sales@fabermusic.com   fabermusicstore.com

CDs recorded at St Paul's Girls' School, Hammersmith, London, June 2008
Piano: Iain Farrington; Language consultants: Tina Ruta, Franziska Roth, Michel Vallat, Ludmilla Andrew
Recorded by Mike Skeet; Produced by Nicola-Jane Kemp and Heidi Pegler
℗ & © 2008 Faber Music Ltd

Pur dicesti, o bocca bella

O beautiful mouth

Antonio Lotti (1667–1740)

Background

Antonio Lotti studied under Giovanni Legrenzi and joined the choir of St Mark's Basilica in Venice where he sang as an alto. He went on to work there in various capacities throughout his life, finally becoming Maestro di Cappella in 1736 until his death. Lotti's music bridges the Baroque and burgeoning Classical styles. He composed in several different genres, including sacred motets (his 'Miserere' is sung in St Mark's to this day), masses and cantatas, madrigals and some thirty operas. Renowned as a teacher, his students included Marcello, Alberti, Bassani, Gasparini, and Galuppi. This aria comes from Act Two of the opera *Arminius* and Auguste Gevaert published it in his collection *Les Gloires de l'Italie* (Paris 1868). Parisotti also included it in his collection of *Arie Antiche* in 1890.

Idiomatic translation

O beautiful lips, you did say that dear, gentle "yes",
which makes my joy complete.
Honouring his flame,
Love opened you, the sweet fountain of delight, with a kiss.

Pronunciation – **Pur dicesti, o bocca bella** [pur ditʃesti o bɔk:ka bɛl:la]

Pur dicesti, o bocca bella,
pur ditʃesti o bɔk:ka bɛl:la

quel soave̯e caro sì,
kwel soave karɔ si

che fa tutto il mio piacer.
ke fa tut:tɔil mio pjatʃer

Per onor di sua facella
per ɔnor di sua fatʃel:la

con un bacio̯Amor t'aprì,
kɔn un batʃɔamor tapri

dolce fonte del goder.
dɔltʃe fɔnte dɛl goder

CD1 spoken text
piano accompaniment

Pur dicesti, o bocca bella
O beautiful mouth

Anonymous

Antonio Lotti
(1667–1740)
arr. Heidi Pegler

p.t.o. for middle section

D.S. 𝄋 al Fine

O del mio dolce ardor bramato oggetto

O desired object of my sweet ardour   Christoph Gluck (1714–87)

Background

Gluck, the son of a forester, was born in Erasbach (then in Czechoslovakia but now in German Bavaria). His passion for music led him to break from his family and travel to pursue his gifts – he studied in Prague and Vienna, and then found his way to Milan and began to compose Italian operas in the *opera seria* and *opera buffa* styles. He finally settled in Vienna, where he became Kapellmeister at the Hapsburg court. As his fame spread, he worked with a young Marie Antoinette in Paris, who became a patron of his. Gluck wrote several French operas in the *opera comique* style. He is, however, best remembered for beginning to challenge the prevailing operatic conventions of the time and developing a more natural dramatic style that was to influence many later composers. The first significant opera in this style was *Orfeo ed Euridice*, performed in Vienna in 1762, followed later by *Paride ed Elena* in 1770 from which this aria comes. In the story from Homer's *Iliad*, Paris was asked to judge which of three goddesses was the most beautiful. His reward for selecting Aphrodite, the goddess of love, was to gain the love of the most beautiful woman in the world – Helen. This song appears at the opening of the opera as Paris arrives on a beach near Sparta and is full of happy anticipation at finally seeing the woman promised to him.

Idiomatic translation

O desired object of my sweet ardour,
at last, the air which you breathe, I breathe.
Wherever I turn my glance, love paints your lovely features in my mind.
My thoughts imagine the most happy hopes,
and in the longing which fills my breast,
I seek you, I call you, I hope and I sigh.

Pronunciation – O del mio dolce ardor bramato oggetto [ɔ dɛl miɔ dɔltʃeardɔr bramatod:ʒet:tɔ]

O del mio dolce ardor
o dɛl miɔ dɔltʃeardɔr

bramato oggetto,
bramatod:ʒet:tɔ

l'aura che tu respiri,
laura ke tu respiri

alfin respiro.
alfin respirɔ

Ovunque il guardo io giro,
ɔvunkwe il gwardɔiɔ dʒirɔ

le tue vaghe sembianze
le tue vage sembjantse

amore in me dipinge:
amɔrein me dipindʒe

Il mio pensier si finge
il miɔ pensjɛr si findʒe

le più liete speranze,
le pju ljɛte sperantse

e nel desio che così
e nɛl deziɔ kɛ kozi

m'empie il petto,
mɛmpje il pet:tɔ

cerco te, chiamo te, spero e sospiro.
tʃɛrkɔ te, kjamɔ te, sperɔ e sɔspirɔ

Further notes

Take care to pronounce every **n** with the tip of the tongue behind the top teeth. An English **ng** as in 'song' [sɔŋ] would not be correct for words such as **finge** or **dipinge** (see the key to Italian pronunciation at the back of this volume).

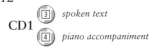

O del mio dolce ardor bramato oggetto

O desired object of my sweet ardour

Raniero de' Calzabigi
(1714–95)

Christoph von Gluck
(1714–87)

arr. Heidi Pegler

* Recording cue

16

at–last I–breathe,

at–last

I–breathe.

* Recording cue

Sovra il campo della vita

Upon the field of life

Gaetano Donizetti (1797–1848)

from *Sei Arie* No. 4

Background

Donizetti was born into a poor and unmusical family in Bergamo, Italy. Musical training in his home town, however, led him to compose operas and he soon found himself with a contract in Naples. His international reputation was finally secured in 1830 with the success of *Anna Bolena*, which was premiered in Milan. Other comic operas were to follow, including *L'Elisir d'amore* and *Don Pasquale*, but his most famous opera is probably the tragedy *Lucia di Lammermoor*, written in 1835 and considered one of the best examples of the *bel canto* tradition. Donizetti is primarily remembered for his operas (around seventy altogether) but he also composed in other genres, including nearly two hundred songs. This one, written around 1844 and dedicated to Catterine Sterlich, comes from the collection *Sei Arie*. Donizetti's family was destined for tragedy: all of his children died young, his wife died of cholera, and he himself descended into mental illness (possibly resulting from syphilis) and spent his final years in mental institutions in Paris and Bergamo.

Idiomatic translation

Upon the field of life
I am an abandoned plant.
I have already wearied of
My immense sorrow.

Without a name, without a fatherland,
I wander, unknown to all peoples.
I look for an echo of my lamentations,
I only find it inside my heart.

Pronunciation – **Sovra il campo della vita** [sovrail kampɔ del:la vita]

Sovra il campo della vita
sovrail   kampɔ del:la vita

sono pianta abbandonata.
sonɔ pjanta ab:bandɔnata

La misura ho già stancata
la mizura ɔ ʤa stankata

dell'immenso mio dolor.
del:lim:mɛnsɔ miɔ dɔlor

Senza nome, senza patria
sentsa nome sentsa patrja

erro ignota a tutte genti.
ɛr:rɔiɲota   a tut:te ʤenti

Cerco un eco a miei lamenti,
tʃɛrkɔun ɛko a mjei lamenti

solo trovo in mezzo al cor.
solɔ trovɔin medzɔal kɔr

Further notes

Note that the pronunciation of the word **mezzo** in Italian has a voiced *z*: [dz].

CD1 [5] *spoken text*
[6] *piano accompaniment*

Sovra il campo della vita

Upon the field of life

Anonymous

Gaetano Donizetti
(1797–1848)

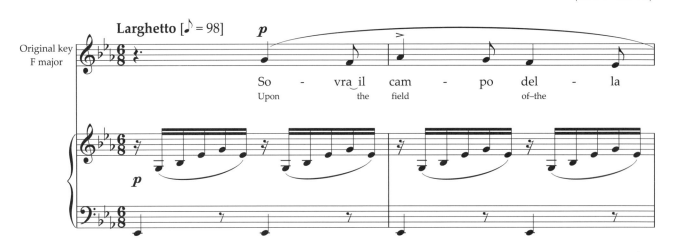

Larghetto [♪ = 98]

Original key
F major

So - vra_il cam - po del - la
Upon   the   field   of–the

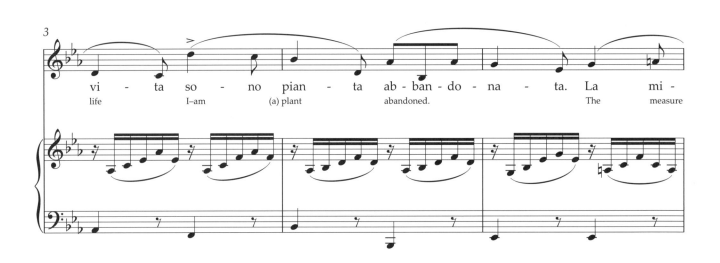

vi - ta so - no pian - ta ab - ban - do - na - ta. La mi -
life   I–am   (a) plant   abandoned.   The   measure

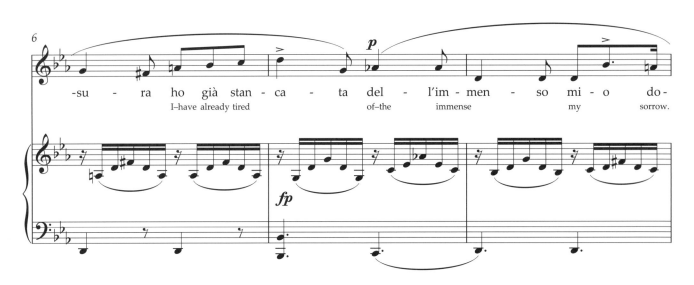

-su - ra ho già stan - ca - ta del - l'im - men - so mi - o do -
I–have already tired   of–the   immense   my   sorrow.

La lontananza

The distance

Gaetano Donizetti (1797–1848)

Background

Donizetti was born into a poor and unmusical family in Bergamo, Italy. Musical training in his home town, however, led him to compose operas and he soon found himself with a contract in Naples. His international reputation was finally secured in 1830 with the success of *Anna Bolena,* which was premiered in Milan. Other comic operas were to follow, including *L'Elisir d'Amore* and *Don Pasquale,* but his most famous opera is probably the tragedy *Lucia di Lammermoor,* written in 1835 and considered one of the best examples of the *bel canto* tradition. Donizetti is primarily remembered for his operas (around seventy altogether) but he also composed in other genres, including nearly two hundred songs. This one, published in 1838, was set to a text by the great operatic librettist Felice Romani, with the style of the piano part suggesting a simple orchestral accompaniment. Donizetti's family was destined for tragedy: all of his children died young, his wife died of cholera, and he himself descended into mental illness (possibly resulting from syphilis) and spent his final years in mental institutions in Paris and Bergamo.

Idiomatic translation

Now that I am stolen from you,
now that you are taken away from me,
I wouldn't substitute the thorns of my life
for another man's flowers.

If a heart is alone in suffering,
that suffering becomes grief,
dear love, dear love.
Oh! dear love!

Pronunciation – La lontananza [la lɔntanantsa]

Or ch'io sono a te rapita,
ɔr kio sonɔa te rapita

or che tolto a me tu sei
ɔr ke tɔltɔa me tu sei

colle spine di mia vita
kɔl:le spine di mia vita

gli altrui fior non cangerei,
ʎaltrui fjɔr non kandʒerei

se a soffrir è solo un core,
sea sɔf:frir ɛ solɔun kɔre

quel soffrir si fa dolore,
kwel sɔf:frir si fa dolore

caro amore, caro amor.
karɔamore karɔamor

Oh! caro amor!
o karɔ amor

La lontananza
The distance

CD1
7 *spoken text*
8 *piano accompaniment*

Felice Romani
(1788–1865)

Gaetano Donizetti
(1797–1848)

Andante ♩. = 58

Original key
F minor

Or ch'io so - no a te ra - pi - ta, or che tol - to a me _ tu
Now that I am from you stolen, now that taken–away from me you

se - i col - le spi - ne di mia vi - ta gli al - trui fior non can - ge - re - i, se a sof-
are with–the thorns of my life the others' flowers not would–I–change, if from

movendo

-frir è so - lo un co - re, quel sof - frir si fa do - lo - re, ca - ro a - mo - re, ca - ro,
suffering is alone a heart, that suffering itself becomes grief, dear love, dear,

* Recording cue

* Recording cue

Teco, sì, vengo anch'io

I am also coming with you, yes

Leonardo Vinci (c.1690–1730)

from *La caduta dei Decemviri*

Background

Neapolitan Leonardo Vinci studied with Gaetano Greco at the Conservatorio dei Poveri di Gesù Cristo in Naples, returning later to become Maestro di Cappella and a teacher of Pergolesi. Although he died mysteriously amidst rumours of poisoning at a relatively young age, he wrote more than twenty successful operas, many in the Neapolitan dialect. *La caduta dei Decemviri* ('The fall of the Decemvirate'), from which this aria comes, was first performed in Naples in 1727. The plot is based on a story recounting the early history of Rome as told by Livy. In 451 BC a commission of ten men (the Decemvirate) was elected to form a means of governing the people but was unsuccessful because one of its members, Claudius Appius, seized power and attempted to rule. In this opera, Appius attempts to gain possession of a young woman, Virginia. She is summoned to appear in court to face false charges of being his escaped slave. In this aria, Icilio, her fiancé, encourages her not to fear, reassuring her that he will protect and not abandon her.

Idiomatic translation

I am also coming with you, yes, and love comes with me.
Have no fear my dear heart, no, have no fear.

Pronunciation – Teco, sì, vengo anch'io [tɛkɔ si vɛngɔ ankiɔ]

Teco, sì, vengo anch'io,
tɛkɔ si vɛngɔankiɔ

e meco viene amor.
e mɛkɔ vjeneamɔr

Non paventar, cor mio,
nɔn paventar kɔr miɔ

nò, non paventar, mio cor.
nɔ nɔn paventar miɔ kɔr

Further notes

The *ng* (as in **vengo**) in Italian lyric diction should not sound like the English *ng* (as in **sing**). See the key to Italian pronunciation at the back of this volume.

Teco, sì, vengo anch'io

I am also coming with you, yes

Silvio Stampiglia
(1664–1725)

Leonardo Vinci
(*c*.1690–1730)
arr. Heidi Pegler

CD1 — spoken text / piano accompaniment

Original key
C major

Te - co, sì,___ ven - go an-ch'i - o, e me - co vie - ne a - mor,___

Te - co, sì,___ ven - go an-ch'i - o, e me - co vie - ne a - mor,___
With-you, yes, come also I, and with-me comes love,

sì, me - co vie - ne a - mor,___ vie - ne a - mor.

sì, me - co vie - ne a - mor, vie - ne a - mor.
yes, with-me comes love, comes love.

sì, me - co vie - ne a - mor,___ vie - ne a - mor.___
yes, with–me comes love, comes love.

FINE

Non pa - ven - tar,___ cor mi - o, nò, non pa - ven - tar, mi - o cor, non pa - ven-
Not to–fear, heart my, no, not to–fear, my heart, not to–fear,

D.C. al Fine
rit.

-tar,_____ nò, non pa - ven - tar,_ mio cor._
no, not to–fear, my heart.

Deh, pietoso, oh Addolorata

Alas, have mercy, oh Virgin of Sorrows
from *Sei Romanze*, No. 6

Guiseppe Verdi (1813–1901)

Background

Verdi was born near the town of Busseto in Italy and is best known as a composer of opera. Many of his works (including *Rigoletto*, *La Traviata*, *Macbeth*, *Otello*, *Aida* and *Falstaff*) form part of the staple repertoire of opera houses today. In 19th-century Italy, the prestige attributed to opera meant that, although popular, other musical forms assumed lesser importance. Such compositions, however, assisted a young composer in raising his profile and prior to his first operatic success with *Nabucco* (1842), Verdi wrote other smaller works, including some instrumental music, sacred motets and songs. This song is the last in a series of six romances (*Sei Romanze*) published in 1838. The Italian text was translated by Luigi Balestri from Goethe's *Faust*: *Ach neige, Du Schmerzensreiche* ('O bend down, you who are full of sorrows'). The primary interest is in the melody with a standard chordal accompaniment, but some of Verdi's dramatic operatic characteristics are foreshadowed in the musical depiction of Gretchen's increasing despair over her doomed love for Faust as she stands before an image of the Virgin Mary.

Idiomatic translation

Alas, have mercy, oh Virgin of Sorrows,
Incline your glance to my sorrow;
You, whose heart is pierced by a sword,
Turn your eyes, desolate one,
Towards your dying son.
Those glances and sighs go
Up to God as a prayer that
Tempers his and your suffering.
As for me, unbearable woes
Tear at my insides,
And who could ever understand

The anxious throbbing in my breast?
Why this trembling heart? What does it want?
Ah! You alone know it, you alone!
Always, whichever step I take,
Whatever torture
I bear here in my breast!
Scarcely alone, oh, how much
I pour out, oh, so much weeping
Bursts inside my heart.
On the vase in the window
My tears fell

When at the morning's dawn
I picked this flower for you,
After the sun's first ray
Lit up my room
And drove me out of bed
With an increasing sorrow.
Ah, by you may I be saved
From dishonour and death.
Oh have mercy on my sorrow
Incline your glance,
Oh Virgin of Sorrows!

Pronunciation – Deh, pietoso, oh Addolorata [dɛ pjetoᵤzɔ o ad:dɔlɔrata]

Deh, pietoso, oh Addolorata,
dɛ pjetoᵤzɔ oad:dɔlɔrata

China il guardo al mio dolore;
kinail gwardɔ al miɔ dolore

Tu, una spada fitta in core,
tu una spada fit:tain cɔre

Volgi gl'occhi desolata
volʤi ʎɔk:ki dezolata

Al morente tuo figliuol.
al morɛnte tuo fiʎuɔl

Quelle occhiate, i sospir vanno
kwel:leɔk:kjatei sospir van:nɔ

Lassù al padre e son preghiera
las:sual padre son pregjera

Che il suo tempri ed il tuo affanno.
keil suᵤo tɛmpried il tuᵤoaf:fan:nɔ

Come a me squarcin le viscere
komea me skwartʃin le viʃere

Gl'insoffribili miei guai
ʎinsof:fribili mjɛi gwai

E dell'ansio petto i palpiti
e del:lansiɔ pɛt:tɔi palpiti

Chi comprendere può mai?
ki komprɛndere pwɔ mai

Di che trema il cor? Che vuol?
di ke tremail kɔr ke vwɔl

Ah! tu sola il sai, tu sol!
a tu sola il sai tu sol

Sempre, ovunque il passo io giro,
sɛmpre ovᵤunkwe il pas:soiᵤo ʤirᵤo

Qual martiro, qual martiro
kwal martirɔ kwal martirɔ

Qui nel sen porto con me!
kwi nel sen pᴐrtᴐ kᴐn me

Solitaria appena, oh, quanto
solitarjap:pena o kwantᴐ

Verso allora, oh, quanto pianto
vɛrsoal:lorao kwantᴐ pjantᴐ

E di dentro scoppia il cor.
e di dɛntrᴐ skᴐp:pjail kᴐr

Sul vasel del finestrino
sul vazel del finestrinᴐ

La mia lacrima scendea
la miᵤa lakrima ʃendᵤea

Quando all'alba del mattino
kwandᴐal:lalba dɛl mat:tinᴐ

Questi fior per te cogliea,
kwesti fjᴐr pɛr te koʎea

Chè del sole il primo raggio
ke dɛl soleil primᴐ rad:ʒᴐ

La mia stanza rischiarava
la miᵤa stantsa riskjarava

E dal letto mi cacciava
e dal lɛt:tᴐ mi katʃava

Agitandomi il dolor.
aʤitandomil dᴐlor

Ah, per te dal disonore,
a pɛr te dal dizᴐnᴐre

Dalla morte io sia salvata.
dal:la mᴐrteiᴐ sia salvata

Deh, pietoso al mio dolore
dɛ pjetozᴐal miᴐ dᴐlor

China il guardo,
kinail gwardᴐ

oh Addolorata!
oad:dᴐlᴐrata

CD1 spoken text
piano accompaniment

Deh, pietoso, oh Addolorata
Alas, have pity, oh Virgin of Sorrows

Wolfgang Goethe
(1749–1832)

Giuseppe Verdi
(1813–1901)

Italian translation by Luigi Balestri (1808–63)

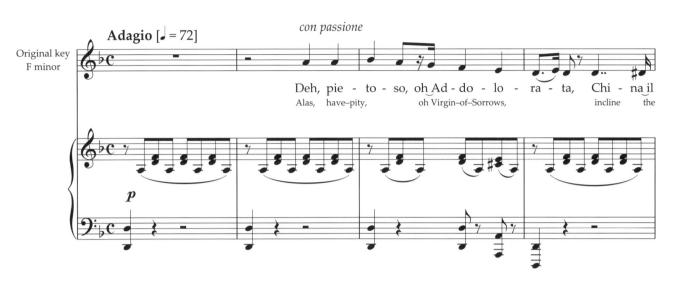

Deh, pie-to-so, oh Ad-do-lo-ra-ta, Chi-na il
Alas, have–pity, oh Virgin–of–Sorrows, incline the

guar-do al mio do-lo-re; Tu, u-na spa-da fit-ta in co-re, Vol-gi
(your) glance to my sorrow; you, a sword driven into (your) heart, turn

gl'oc-chi de-so-la-ta Al mo-ren-te tuo fi-gliuol. Quelle oc-
the (your) eyes desolate-one to-the dying-one your son. Those glances

* Recording cue

* Recording cue

Mattinata

Morning   **Ruggiero Leoncavallo (1857–1919)**

Background

Ruggiero Leoncavallo was born in Naples. Although his father was a judge, he shunned a career in the law and went into opera as a librettist and composer, studying music at the Conservatorio San Pietro a Majella in Naples and literature at Bologna University. His first big success came with the opera *Pagliacci*, performed in Milan in 1892 and written in the 'verismo' style – a movement that aimed to depict contemporary life, especially the life of the lower classes, in all its violent and sometimes sordid realism. Leoncavallo wrote other operas in his lifetime, but today he is principally remembered for *Pagliacci*, his libretto for Puccini's opera *Manon Lescaut* and this song, recorded by the great tenor Enrico Caruso in 1904.

Idiomatic translation

The dawn, dressed in white,
is opening her door to the great sun,
and with rosy fingers
caresses the multitude of flowers.
All creation appears to be
moved by a mysterious quiver,

yet you will not wake up, and in vain
I stand here sadly and sing.
You also, put on your white dress
and open the door to your singer!
Wherever you are not, light is absent;
wherever you are, love is born!

Pronunciation – **Mattinata** [mat:tinata]

L'aurora, di bianco vestita,
laurọra di bjanko vestịta

già l'uscio dischiude al gran sol,
ʤa luʃɔ diskjudeal gran sol

di già, con le rosee sue dita
di ʤa kɔn le rọze suẹ dịta

carezza de' fiori lo stuol!
karẹt:tsa de fjọri lo stwọl

Commosso da un fremito arcano
kɔm:mọs:sɔ daun fremitɔarkạnɔ

intorno il creato già par,
intọrnɔil kreạtɔ ʤa par

e tu non ti desti, ed invano
e tu nɔn ti dẹsti ed invạnɔ

mi sto qui dolente a cantar.
mi stɔ kwi dɔlẹntea kantạr

Metti anche tu la veste bianca
mẹt:tianke tu la vẹste bjanka

e schiudi l'uscio al tuo cantor!
e skjudi lụʃɔ al tụɔ kantọr

Ove non sei la luce manca,
ọve nɔn sẹi la lụtʃe manka

ove tu sei nasce l'amor!
ọve tu sẹi naʃe lamọr

Further notes

The consonant combination ...**schi** is pronounced [ski]. Take care not to insert the English sound ...*ng* into words such as *bianco* or *manca*. The *n* is formed with the tip of the tongue behind the top teeth (see the key to Italian pronunciation at the back of this volume). Note that **desti** (wake up) must be pronounced with an open *e* [ɛ] to avoid confusion with **desti** [desti], which means 'you gave'.

Mattinata
Morning

CD1 [13] *spoken text*
[14] *piano accompaniment*

Ruggiero Leoncavallo
(1857–1919)

Ruggiero Leoncavallo
(1857–1919)
arr. Heidi Pegler

tu la ve-ste bian-ca e schiu - di l'u - scio al tuo can-
you the dress white and open the door to your singer!

-tor! O - ve non se - i la lu - ce man - ca, o - ve tu
Where not you–are the light lacks, where you

se - i nas-ce l'a - mor!
are is–born the love!

Widmung

Dedication

from *Myrthen*

Robert Schumann (1810–56) Op. 25 No. 1

Background

'Widmung' is the first song in the cycle *Myrthen, Liederkreis* ('Myrtles, Song-cycle'), which comprises twenty-six songs composed by Schumann in February 1840 as a wedding present for his beloved Clara Wieck. The pair were forcibly separated by Clara's father, who opposed their union, and the song-cycle recollects the joy and pain of love, and being apart. The text is taken from a poem by Friedrich Rückert (1788–1866), which conveys the idea of the transforming power of love between a man and a woman. It is one of several themes concerning relationships that Schumann explores throughout the cycle and it also contains some specially hidden ciphers and messages that Schumann and Clara secretly shared between them.

Idiomatic translation

You my soul, you my heart,
you my joy, O you my pain,
you the world in which I live,
you my heaven, in which I float,
O you my grave, into which
I forever lay down my grief.

You are tranquillity, you are peace,
Heaven has bestowed you upon me.
That you love me gives me my worth,
your gaze transfigures me,
you raise me lovingly above myself,
my good spirit, my better self!

Pronunciation – **Widmung** [vɪtmʊŋ]

Du meine Seele, du mein Herz,
duː maɪnə zeːlə duː maɪn hɛrts

du meine Wonn', o du mein Schmerz,
duː maɪnə vɔn |oː duː maɪn ʃmɛrts

du meine Welt, in der ich lebe,
duː maɪnə vɛlt |ɪn deːɐ |ɪç leːbə

mein Himmel du, darein ich schwebe,
maɪn hɪməl duː daraɪn |ɪç ʃveːbə

o du mein Grab, in das hinab
|oː duː maɪn grap |ɪn das hɪnap

ich ewig meinen Kummer gab!
|ɪç |eːvɪç maɪnən kʊmɐ gaːp

Du bist die Ruh', du bist der Frieden,
duː bɪst diː ruː duː bɪst deːɐ friːdən

du bist vom Himmel mir beschieden.
duː bɪst fɔm hɪməl miːɐ bəʃiːdən

Daß du mich liebst, macht mich mir wert,
das duː mɪç liːbst maxt mɪç miːɐ veːrt

dein Blick hat mich vor mir verklärt,
daɪn blɪk hat mɪç foːɐ miːɐ fɛɐkleːrt

du hebst mich liebend über mich,
duː heːbst mɪç liːbənt |yːbɐ mɪç

mein guter Geist, mein bess'res Ich!
maɪn guːtɐ gaɪst, maɪn bɛsrəs |ɪç

CD1 15 *spoken text*
16 *piano accompaniment*

Widmung
Dedication

Friedrich Rückert
(1788–1866)

Robert Schumann Op. 25 No. 1
(1810–56)

Original key
A♭ major

Innig, lebhaft *(heartfelt, lively)* [♩ = 69]

Du mei-ne See - le, du mein
You my soul, you my

Herz, du mei-ne Wonn', o du mein Schmerz, du mei-ne
heart, you my joy, o you my pain, you my

Welt, in der ich le - be, mein Him-mel du, dar-ein ich
world, in which I live, my heaven you, into-it I

Du bist die Ruh

You are rest   Franz Schubert (1797–1828) Op. 59 No. 3 D776

Background

This song, written in 1823, was published in 1826 as part of a collection entitled *Four Songs by Rückert and Graf Platen*. The text comes from *Östliche Rosen* ('Oriental Roses'), a collection of untitled poems, the name of which Schubert chose himself. He sets this poem in a simple, almost religious expression of selfless love.

Idiomatic translation

You are rest, the gentle peace,
you are longing and what stills it.
I dedicate to you full of joy and pain
as a dwelling here my eyes and heart.

Come in to me, and close
the door quietly behind you.
Drive other pain from this breast!
May my heart be filled with your joy.

This canopy of my eyes is lit up
by your radiance alone. O fill it completely.

Pronunciation – **Du bist die Ruh** [duː bɪst diː ruː]

Du bist die Ruh, der Friede mild,
duː bist diː ruː   deːɐ friːdə mɪlt

Kehr ein bei mir, und schließe du
keːr |ain bai miːɐ |ʊnt ʃliːsə   duː

die Sehnsucht du, und was sie stillt.
diː zeːnzʊxt   duː |ʊnt vas ziː ʃtɪlt

still hinter dir die Pforten zu.
ʃtɪl hɪntɐ diːɐ diː pfɔrtən tsuː

 Ich weihe dir voll Lust und Schmerz
|ɪç vaːiə diːɐ fɔl lʊst |ʊnt ʃmɛrts

Treib andern Schmerz aus dieser Brust!
traip |andern ʃmɛrts |aus diːzɐ brʊst

zur Wohnung hier mein Aug und Herz.
tsuːɐ voːnʊŋ   hiːɐ main |auk |ʊnt hɛrts

Voll sei dies Herz von deiner Lust.
fɔl   zai diːs hɛrts fɔn dainɐ lʊst

Dies Augenzelt, von deinem Glanz
diːs |augəntselt fɔn dainəm glants

 allein erhellt, o füll es ganz.
|alain |ɛɐhɛlt |oː fʏl |ɛs gants

17 *spoken text*
18 *piano accompaniment*

Du bist die Ruh
You are rest

Friedrich Rückert
(1788–1866)

Franz Schubert Op. 59 No. 3 D776
(1797–1828)

Original key
E♭ major

Du bist die Ruh, der Frie - de mild, die Sehn - sucht du, und was sie stillt.
You are the calm, the peace mild, the longing you, and what it stills.

Ich wei - he dir____ voll Lust_ und_ Schmerz zur Woh - nung hier____
I dedicate to–you full (of) joy and pain as–the dwelling here

mein_ Aug_ und_ Herz,____ mein Aug_ und_ Herz.
my eye and heart, my eye and heart.

Verborgenheit

Seclusion

Hugo Wolf (1860–1903) M12

Background

Hugo Wolf learned the piano and violin as a child, and became a music critic in Vienna at the age of twenty-four. A combination of the effects of syphilis and a bi-polar temperament resulted in difficulties sustaining relationships and regular work. Nevertheless, at twenty-eight he entered a swift (and all too short) period of intense creative activity, composing over two hundred songs between 1888 and 1891. Dying tragically early of syphilitic mental deterioration at the age of forty-three, his final years included brief outbursts of great compositional activity, composing up to three songs in a day at times, and long years of silence in between. He wrote an opera and some instrumental music, but he is primarily remembered for his immense legacy of Lieder. 'Verborgenheit' (1888) comes from a collection of settings by the pastor, artist and poet Eduard Mörike, whose themes explore the heights and depths of everyday life, and in this case, of love's conflicting emotions – something that Wolf himself may have closely identified with.

Idiomatic translation

Let, o world, o let me be!
Do not tempt me with gifts of love,
Leave this heart alone to feel
Its delight, its pain!

I know not why I grieve,
It is unknown woe;
Constantly, through tears
I see the sun's dear light.

Often, I am hardly aware,
And bright joy quivers
Through the heaviness that oppresses me,
Delighting my heart.

Let, o world, etc. ...

Pronunciation – Verborgenheit [fɛɐbɔrgənhait]

Laß, o Welt, o laß mich sein!
las |oː vɛlt |oː las mɪç zain

Locket nicht mit Liebesgaben,
lɔkət nɪçt mɪt liːbəsgaːbən

Laßt dies Herz alleine haben
last diːs hɛrts |alainə haːbən

Seine Wonne, seine Pein!
zainə vɔnə, zainə pain

Was ich traure, weiß ich nicht,
vas |ɪç traurə vais |ɪç nɪçt

Es ist unbekanntes Wehe;
|ɛs |ɪst |unbəkantəs veːə

Immerdar durch Tränen sehe
|ımɐdar durç* trɛːnən seːə

Ich der Sonne liebes Licht.
|ɪç deːɐ zɔnə liːbəs lɪçt

Oft bin ich mir kaum bewußt,
|ɔft bɪn |ɪç miːɐ kaum bəvust

Und die helle Freude zücket
|unt diː hɛlə frɔidə tsʏkət

Durch die Schwere, so mich drücket
durç diː ʃverə zoː mɪç drʏkət

Wonniglich in meiner Brust.
vɔnɪklɪç |ın mainɐ brust

Laß, o Welt, ...etc
las |oː vɛlt

Further notes

Ensure that the *ch* [ç] sounds are correctly pronounced. They are all the same in this song.

* The word **durch** is problematic for English speakers. Practise saying [dur – ıç], then leave out the [ı] – [dur – ç], then bring the two sounds closer together. In bar 15 however, the word **durch** is of such short duration that it is better to omit the *r* and replace it with [ɐ], thus pronouncing it [durɐç]. Note also that in German, where words ending in *-ig* have the suffix *-lich*, the *g* is hardened to a *k*. For example, **wonniglich** is pronounced [vɔnɪklɪç].

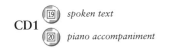

CD1

19 spoken text

20 piano accompaniment

Verborgenheit
Seclusion

Eduard Mörike
(1804–75)

Hugo Wolf M12
(1860–1903)

Mässig und sehr innig *(Moderate and very heartfelt)* [♩ = 60]

Original key
E♭ major

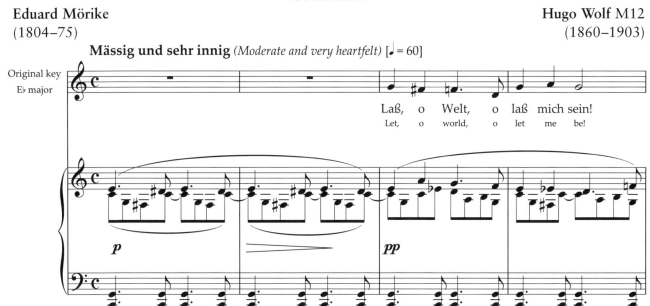

Laß, o Welt, o laß mich sein!
Let, o world, o let me be!

Lo - cket nicht mit Lie - bes - ga - ben, Laßt dies Herz al - lei - ne ha - ben
Tempt (me) not with love's–gifts, let this heart alone to–have

Sei - ne Won - ne, sei - ne Pein! Was ich trau - re, weiß ich nicht,___
its delight, its pain! What I mourn, know I not,

nach und nach belebter und leidenschaftlicher
(gradually more animated and passionate)

Du bist wie eine Blume

You are like a flower   Robert Schumann (1810–56) Op. 25 No. 24

Background

Like 'Widmung', which appears earlier in this volume, 'Du bist wie eine Blume' comes from the cycle *Myrthen, Liederkries* ('Myrtles, Song-cycle'), which consists of twenty-six songs composed by Schumann in February 1840 as a wedding present for his beloved Clara Wieck. Of all Heine's poems, its direct simplicity and intimacy has led to it being set by more composers than any other. As with 'Widmung' and others in this cycle, 'Clara themes' are hidden in the accompaniment and elsewhere, and this song was apparently a particular favourite of Clara's.

Idiomatic translation

You are like a flower,
so dear and beautiful and pure;
I look at you and melancholy
steals into my heart.

I feel as if I should lay
my hands upon your head,
praying that God preserves you
so pure and beautiful and dear.

Pronunciation – **Du bist wie eine Blume** [duː bɪst viː |ainə bluːmə]

Du bist wie eine Blume,
duː bist viː |ainə bluːmə

so hold und schön und rein;
zoː hɔlt |ʊnt ʃøːn |ʊnt rain

ich schau' dich an, und Wehmut
|ɪç ʃau dɪç |an |ʊnt veːmuːt

schleicht mir in's Herz hinein.
ʃlaiçt miːɐ |ins hɛrts hɪnain

Mir ist, als ob ich die Hände
miːɐ |ist |als |ɔp |ɪç diː hɛndə

auf's Haupt dir legen sollt',
|aufs haupt diːɐ leːgən zɔlt

betend, daß Gott dich erhalte
beːtənt das gɔt dɪç |ɛɐhaltə

so rein und schön und hold.
zoː rain |ʊnt ʃøːn |ʊnt hɔlt

Du bist wie eine Blume

You are like a flower

CD1 21 spoken text
22 piano accompaniment

Heinrich Heine
(1797–1856)

Robert Schumann Op. 25 No. 24
(1810–56)

Original key
A♭ major

54

Die Mainacht

The May night   Johannes Brahms (1833–97) Op. 43 No. 2

Background

Ludwig Hölty was considered one of the most important German poets of the 18th century after Goethe. His poems are suffused with a melancholy that attracted Brahms, who set several of his poems. The original texts were edited considerably by JH Voss (published 1804) and in this poem, Brahms omits the second stanza. This song was written in 1866 and evokes a common theme – that of the lonely outsider. This poem is full of symbolism. The moon at the start sets up a feeling of uncertainty and change. The nightingale indicates love but the doves are unusual because they rarely appear at night. The dark shadows represent a confusion of feelings and a sense of unfulfilled and hopeless love.

Idiomatic translation

When the silvery moon gleams through the shrubs,
and casts its slumbering light over the lawn,
and the nightingale sings,
I wander sadly from bush to bush.

Enveloped by foliage, a pair of doves
coo their delight to me.
But I turn away, seeking darker shadows,
and a lone tear flows.

When, o smiling image that like the red of dawn
Shines through my soul, shall I find you on earth?
And the lonely tear trembles,
More hotly, down my cheek.

Pronunciation – **Die Mainacht** [di: mainaxt]

Wann der silberne Mond durch die Gesträuche blinkt,
van   deːɐ zɪlbɐnə moːnt dʊrç di: ɡəʃtrɔiçə   blɪnkt

und sein schlummerndes Licht über den Rasen streut,
|ʊnt zain ʃlʊmɐndəs   lɪçt |yːbɐ deːn raːzən ʃtrɔit

und die Nachtigall flötet,
|ʊnt di: naxtigal   fløːtət

wandl' ich traurig von Busch zu Busch.
vandlɪç   traurɪç fɔn bʊʃ   tsu: bʊʃ

Überhüllet vom Laub, girret ein Taubenpaar
|yːbɐhylət fɔm laup gɪrət |ain taubənpaːr

sein Entzücken mir vor;
zain |ɛntsykən miːɐ foːɐ

aber ich wende mich, suche dunklere Schatten,
|abɐ |ɪç vɛndə mɪç   zuːxə dʊnklərə ʃatən

und die einsame Träne rinnt.
|ʊnt di: |ainzaːmə trɛːnə rɪnt

Wann, o lächelndes Bild, welches wie Morgenrot
van |o: lɛçɛlndəs bɪlt vɛlçəs vi: mɔrgənroːt

durch die Seele mir strahlt, find' ich auf Erden dich?
dʊrç di: zeːlə miːɐ ʃtraːlt fɪnd |ɪç |auf |eːrdən dɪç

Und die einsame Träne bebt mir heißer,
|ʊnt di: |ainzamə trɛːnə beːbt miːɐ haisɐ

heißer die Wang' herab.
haisɐ di: vaŋ   hɛrap

Further notes

Durch is a difficult word for some English speakers. Practise saying [dʊr – ɪç], then leave out the [ɪ] – [dʊr – ç], then bring the two sounds closer together. Note also that there is no glottal stop between the words **wandl'** and **ich**. The medial *r* in **silberne** and **schlummerndes** is not pronounced here to encourage a smoother line in this atmospheric opening. However, this is open to individual artistic interpretation.

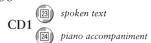

Die Mainacht
The May night

Ludwig Hölty
(1748–76)

Johannes Brahms Op. 43 No. 2
(1833–97)

Busch.
bush.

Ü - ber - hül - let vom
Enveloped by–the

Laub, gir - ret ein Tau - ben-paar sein Ent - zü - cken mir
foliage, coos a dove–pair their delight to–me;

vor; a - ber ich
but I

wen - de mich, su - che dunk - le - re
turn–away myself, seek darker

Und die ein- sa- me Trä- - -
And the lonely tear

- ne bebt mir hei- ßer,
trembles to—me hotter,

hei- - ßer die Wang' her-
hotter the cheek down.

- ab.

Die beiden Grenadiere

The two grenadiers   Robert Schumann (1810–56) Op. 49 No. 1

Background

Alongside the works of Goethe, the poems of Heinrich Heine form an integral part of German art song and have been set by many composers. Most of the texts come from his collection *Buch der Lieder* (Book of Songs) of 1827 and have a common theme of unrequited love. This poem, however, appears in a set of twenty *Romanzen*, consisting of short ballads telling descriptive stories. Schumann set four of these in 1840 and this text reflects Heine's experience as a young man, seeing French soldiers returning from the war with Russia in 1816, which he supposedly witnessed while living in Dusseldorf. Schumann expertly weaves in the *Marseillaise* at the moment of the soldier's visionary resurrection, though it is clear from the piano postlude that the soldier ultimately loses his life.

Idiomatic translation

Two grenadiers, captured in Russia,
Were returning to France.
And as they crossed into German territory
They hung their heads.

For both heard there the sorry tale
That France was lost and gone,
Her valiant army beaten and defeated –
And the Emperor, the Emperor captured.

The grenadiers then wept together
As they heard of the sad news.
The first said: "Ah, the agony,
How my old wound is burning!"

The second said: "The song is over,
I would die with you also,
But I've a wife and child at home,
Who without me would perish."

"What care I for a wife, what care I for a child,
I have a nobler desire:
Let them beg, if they are hungry –
My Emperor, my Emperor captured!

Grant me, brother, one favour:
If I am now to die,
Take my corpse with you to France,
Bury me in French soil.

You shall lay on my heart
The Cross of Honour with its red ribbon;
And place my musket in my hand
And gird my sword about me.

So shall I lie and listen silently
Like a sentry in my grave,
Until I hear the cannons' roar
And the horses gallop and neigh.

My Emperor will then ride over my grave,
Many swords clashing and flashing;
I shall then rise armed from the grave –
To protect the Emperor, my Emperor."

Pronunciation – Die beiden Grenadiere [diː baidən grenadiːrə]

Nach Frankreich zogen zwei Grenadier',
naːx frankraiç tsoːgən tsvai grenadiːɐ

die waren in Rußland gefangen.
diː vaːrən |ɪn rʊslant gəfaŋən

Und als sie kamen ins deutsche Quartier,
|ʊnt |als ziː kaːmən |ɪns doitʃə kvartiːɐ

sie ließen die Köpfe hangen.
ziː liːsən diː kœpfə haŋən

Da hörten sie beide die traurige Mär':
da høːrtən ziː baidə diː traurɪgə mɛːɐ

daß Frankreich verloren gegangen,
das frankraiç fɛɐloːrən gəgaŋən

besiegt und geschlagen das tapfere Heer,
bəziːkt |ʊnt gəʃlaːgən   das tapfərə heːɐ

und der Kaiser, gefangen.
|ʊnt deːɐ kaizɐ gəfaŋən

"Was schert mich Weib, was schert mich Kind,
vas ʃeːɐt mɪç vaip vas ʃeːɐt mɪç kɪnt

ich trage weit besser Verlangen;
|ɪç traːgə vait bɛsɐ fɛɐlaŋən

so nimm meine Leiche nach Frankreich mit,
zoː nɪm mainə laiçə naːx frankraiç mɪt

begrab' mich in Frankreichs Erde.
bəgraːp mɪç |ɪn frankraiçs |eːrdə

laß sie betteln gehn, wenn sie hunrig sind, –
las ziː bɛtɛln geːn vɛn ziː hʊnrɪç zɪnt

mein Kaiser, mein Kaiser gefangen!
main kaizɐ main kaizɐ gəfaŋən

Gewähr' mir, Bruder, eine Bitt':
gəveːr   miːɐ bruːdɐ |ainə bɪt

Wenn ich jetzt sterben werde,
vɛn |ɪç jɛtst ʃteːrbən veːrdə

Da weinten zusammen die Grenadier'
da vaintən tsuːzamən diː grenadiːɐ

wohl ob der kläglichen Kunde.
voːl |ɔp deːɐ klɛːklɪçən kʊndə

Der eine sprach: "Wie weh' wird mir,
deːɐ |ainə ʃpraːx viː veː vɪɐt miːɐ

wie brennt meine alte Wunde!"
viː brɛnt mainə |altə vʊndə

Der andre sprach: "Das Lied ist aus,
deːɐ |andrə ʃpraːx das liːt |ɪst |aus

 auch ich möcht' mit dir sterben,
|aux |ɪç mœçt mɪt diːɐ ʃtɛrbən

doch hab' ich Weib und Kind zu Haus,
dɔx hap |ɪç vaip |ʊnt kɪnt tsuː haus

die ohne mich verderben."
diː |oːnə mɪç fɛɐdɛrbən

Das Ehrenkreuz am roten Band
das |eːrənkroits |am roːtən bant

sollst du aufs Herz mir legen;
zɔlst duː |aufs hɛrts miːɐ leːgən

die Flinte gib mir in die Hand,
diː flɪntə gɪp miːɐ |ɪn diː hant

 und gürt' mir um den Degen.
|ʊnt gʏrt miːɐ |ʊm deːn deːgən

So will ich liegen und horchen still,
zoː vɪl |ɪç liːgən |ʊnt hɔrçən ʃtɪl

wie eine Schildwach', im Grabe,
viː |ainə ʃɪltvax |ɪm graːbə

bis einst ich höre Kanonengebrüll
bɪs |ainst |ɪç høːrə kanoːnəngəbrʏl

 und wiehernder Rosse Getrabe.
|ʊnt viːɐndɐ rɔsə gətraːbə

Dann reitet mein Kaiser wohl über mein Grab,
dan raitət main kaizɐ voːl |yːbɐ main grap

viel Schwerter klirren und blitzen;
fiːl ʃveːrtɐ klɪrən |ʊnt blɪtsən

dann steig' ich gewaffnet hervor aus dem Grab –
dan ʃtaig |ɪç gəvafnət hɛrfoːɐ |aus deːm grap

den Kaiser, den Kaiser zu schütze n!"
deːn kaizɐ deːn kaizɐ tsuː ʃʏtsən

Further notes

Note that the pronunciation of the first syllable of the word **Grenadier'** has a closed [e] but without the usual lengthening [eː]. This is due to the foreign origin of the word. In German, when singing at speed, or for artistic reasons, some final consonants are left out or absorbed into the initial consonant of the following word. For example, in this song, **sollst du** and **und der** should be joined in a similar way to our English phrase 'shut down'.

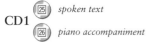

Die beiden Grenadiere

The two grenadiers

Heinrich Heine
(1797–1856)

Robert Schumann Op. 49 No. 1
(1810–56)

Von ewiger Liebe

Of eternal love   Johannes Brahms (1833–97) Op. 43 No. 1

Background

The poet Hoffmann was dismissed from his post as Professor of German Language and Literature at Breslau University after professing his views in support of German unity. His 'Deutschland, Deutschland über alles' (Germany, Germany over everything) became the national anthem. This poem, taken from his *Gedichte* (Poems) of 1837, was also set by Schumman. The link is significant as Brahms held a long passion for Schumann's wife, the pianist and composer Clara Schumann, and was a frequent visitor to the family home. It is reported by Kalbeck that when Brahms performed this song for Clara, she sat silently weeping. The great Lieder composer Hugo Wolf, who was no fan of Brahms, said of this song that it should be considered his masterpiece. The poem is full of symbolism and bold imagery. The wood indicates a place of free love, but the darkness depicts confusion and frustration of feelings. Even the lark, a bird symbolising love, is silent. The boy escorts his beloved past a willow copse, which indicates separation or parting. Here is a love that is not approved of by others, but the boy and girl promise that their love will hold strong and steadfast forever.

Idiomatic translation

Dark, how dark in forest and field!
It is evening already, now the world is silent.
Nowhere remains a light and nowhere smoke,
Yes, even the lark is silent now too.

Out of the village there comes a young lad,
Escorting his beloved home.
He leads her past the willow copse,
Talking too much and of so many things:

"If you suffer shame and become distressed,
If you suffer shame from what others think of me,
Then let our love be dissolved as swiftly,
As swiftly as we were united before.
Let us separate with rain and separate with wind,
As swiftly as we were united before."

The girl speaks, the girl says:
"Our love cannot be dissolved!
Steel is strong, and iron even more so.
Our love is stronger still:

Iron and steel can both be re-forged,
But our love, who shall change it?
Iron and steel can be melted down;
Our love must for ever endure!"

Pronunciation – **Von ewiger Liebe** [fɔn ˈeːvɪɡɐ liːbə]

Dunkel, wie dunkel in Wald und in Feld!
dʊŋkəl viː dʊŋkəl ˈɪn valt ˈʊnt ˈɪn fɛlt

 Abend schon ist es, nun schweiget die Welt.
ˈabənt ʃon ˈɪst ˈɛs nʊn ʃvaigət diː vɛlt

Nirgend noch Licht und nirgend noch Rauch,
nɪrgənt nɔx lɪxt ˈʊnt nɪrgənt nɔx raux

ja, und die Lerche sie schweiget nun auch.
jaː ˈʊnt diː lɛrçə ziː ʃvaigət nuːn ˈaux

"Leidest du Schmach und betrübest du dich,
  laidəst duː ʃmaːx ˈʊnt bətryːbəst duː dɪç

leidest du Schmach von andern um mich,
laidəst duː ʃmaːx fɔn ˈandern ˈʊm mɪç

werde die Liebe getrennt so geschwind,
veːrdə diː liːbə gətrɛnt zoː gəʃvɪnt

schnell wie wir früher vereiniget sind.
ʃnɛl viː viːɐ fryːɐ fɛɐˈainɪgət zɪnt

Scheide mit Regen und scheide mit Wind,
ʃaidə mɪt reːgən ˈʊnt ʃaidə mɪt vɪnt

Schnell wie wir früher vereiniget sind."
ʃnɛl viː viːɐ fryːɐ fɛɐˈainɪgət zɪnt

68

Kommt aus dem Dorfe der Bursche heraus,
kɔmt |aus deːm dɔrfə deːʁ burʃə hɛraus

gibt das Geleit der Geliebten nach Haus,
gɪbt das gəlait deːʁ gəliːptən naːx haus

führt sie am Weidengebüsche vorbei,
fyːrt ziː |am viːdəngəbyʃə foʁbai

redet so viel und so mancherlei:
reːdət zoː fiːl |unt zoː mançʁlai

Spricht das Mägdelein, Mägdelein spricht:
ʃprɪçt das mɛːkdəlain mɛːkdəlain ʃprɪçt

"Unsere Liebe sie trennet sich nicht!
|unzərə liːbə ziː trɛnət zɪç nɪçt

Fest ist der Stahl und das Eisen gar sehr,
fɛst |ɪst deːʁ ʃtaːl |unt das |aizən gaː zeːʁ

unsere Liebe ist fester noch mehr.
|unzərə liːbə |ɪst fɛstʁ nɔx meːʁ

Eisen und Stahl, man schmiedet sie um,
|aizən |unt ʃtaːl man ʃmiːdət ziː |um

unsere Liebe, wer wandelt sie um?
|unzərə liːbə veːʁ vandɛlt ziː |um

Eisen und Stahl, sie können zergehn,
|aizən |unt ʃtaːl ziː kœnən tsɛʁgeːn

unsere Liebe, muß ewig bestehn!"
|unzərə liːbə mus |eːvɪç bəʃteːn

Further notes

Note the mid-word glottal stop in **vereiniget** [fɛʁlainɪgət]. In German, when singing at speed, or for artistic reasons, some final consonants are left out or absorbed into the initial consonant of the following word. For example, in this song, **und das** and **betrübest du** should be joined in a similar way to our English phrase 'shut down'. Similarly, the r in **gar** is implied but not rolled. Listen to the CD carefully.

Von ewiger Liebe
Of eternal love

CD1
[27] spoken text
[28] piano accompaniment

August Heinrich Hoffmann von Fallersleben
(1798–1874)

Johannes Brahms Op. 43 No. 1
(1833–97)

© 2008 by Faber Music Ltd

72

Les roses d'Ispahan

The roses of Isfahan   Gabriel Fauré (1845–1924) Op. 39 No. 4

Background

This setting of a poem by Leconte de Lisle (1818–94) was composed in 1884, and forms part of the second collection of Fauré's songs published by Hamelle. De Lisle was the leading light amongst a group of poets known as the Parnassians, who emphasised clarity and form in their works, often choosing exotic or classical subjects, rich in colourful imagery, which were then treated with a certain objectivity and detachment. Here, the rocking movement of the piano accompaniment evokes the swaying journey of the traveller, and the harmonies conjure up the sultry heat of Persia.

Idiomatic translation

The roses of Isfahan in their sheath of moss,
the jasmines of Mosul, the orange blossoms,
have a perfume less fresh, a fragrance less sweet,
o pale Leila, than your soft breath!

Your lips are coral and your light laughter
sounds better than running water, and has a voice more sweet.
Better than the joyous breeze that rocks the orange-tree,
better than the bird that sings on the edge of its nest of moss.

O Leila, ever since in their airy flight
all the kisses have fled from your lips so sweet,
there is no longer any fragrance from the pale orange-tree,
no heavenly aroma from the roses in the moss.

Oh, that your youthful love, that light butterfly,
would return to my heart on swift and sweet wings
and perfume once more the orange blossom
and the roses of Isfahan in their sheath of moss.

Pronunciation – Les roses d'Ispahan [lɛ ʀoz dispaɑ̃]

Les roses d'Ispahan dans leur gaîne de mousse,
lɛ ʀozə dispaɑ̃   dɑ̃   lœʀ gɛnə də musə

Les jasmins de Mossoul, les fleurs de l'oranger,
lɛ ʒasmɛ̃ də mɔsul   lɛ flœʀ də lɔʀɑ̃ʒe

Ont un parfum moins frais, | ont une odeur moins douce,
ɔ̃(t)œ̃ paʀfœ̃ mwɛ̃ fʀɛ   ɔ̃(t)ynɔdœʀ   mwɛ̃ dusə

Ô blanche Leïlah! que ton souffle léger.
o blɑ̃ʃə   Leila kə tɔ̃ suflə leʒe

Ta lèvre est de corail et ton rire léger
ta lɛvʀə   də kɔʀaj e tɔ̃ ʀiʀə leʒe

Sonne mieux que l'eau vive et d'une voix plus douce,
sɔnə mjø kə lo vive dynə vwa ply dusə

Mieux que le vent joyeux qui berce l'oranger,
mjø   kə lə vɑ̃ ʒwajø ki bɛʀsə lɔʀɑ̃ʒe

Mieux que l'oiseau qui chante au bord d'un nid de mousse.
mjø   kə lwazo ki ʃɑ̃to   bɔʀ dœ̃ ni də musə

Ô Leïlah! depuis que de leur vol léger
o leila   dəpɥi kə də lœʀ vɔl leʒe

Tous les baisers | ont fui de ta lèvre si douce,
tu lɛ beze   ɔ̃ fɥi də ta lɛvʀə si dusə

Il n'est plus de parfum dans le pâle oranger,
il nɛ   ply də paʀfœ̃ dɑ̃ le palɔʀɑ̃ʒe

Ni de céleste arôme aux roses dans leur mousse.
ni də selɛstaʀomo   ʀozə dɑ̃   lœʀ musə

Oh! que ton jeune amour, ce papillon léger,
o   kə tɔ̃ ʒœnamuʀ   sə papijɔ̃ leʒe

Revienne vers mon cœur d'une aile prompte et douce,
ʀəvjɛnə vɛʀ mɔ̃ kœʀ dynɛlə   pʀɔ̃te   dusə

Et qu'il parfume encor la fleur de l'oranger,
e kil paʀfymɑ̃kɔʀ la flœʀ də lɔʀɑ̃ʒe

Les roses d'Ispahan dans leur gaine de mousse.
lɛ ʀozə dispaɑ̃ dɑ̃ lœʀ gɛnə də musə

Further notes

In the word **prompte** the second *p* is silent.

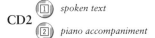

CD2 ① *spoken text*
② *piano accompaniment*

Les roses d'Ispahan
The roses of Isfahan

Charles-Marie-René Leconte de Lisle
(1818–94)

Gabriel Fauré Op. 39 No. 4
(1845–1924)

Les ro - ses d'Is-pa - han dans leur gaî - ne de mous - se, Les jas -
The roses of Isfahan in their covering of moss, the

- mins de Mos - soul, les fleurs de l'o - ran - ger,
jasmines of Mosul, the flowers of the orange-tree,

Ont un par-fum moins frais, ont u - ne o-deur moins dou - ce, Ô blan - che
have a perfume less fresh, have a fragrance less sweet, o white

Le - ï - lah! que ton souf - fle lé - ger.
Leilah! than your breath light.

Ta lè - vre est de co - rail et ton ri - re lé - ger Son - ne
Your lip is of coral and your laugh light sounds

mieux que l'eau vi - ve et d'u - ne voix plus dou - ce,
better than [the] water live and of a voice more sweet,

Mieux que le vent joy - eux qui ber - ce l'o - ran - ger, Mieux que l'oi - seau qui
better than the wind joyful that rocks the orange-tree, better than the bird who

Les berceaux

The cradles　　　　　　　　　　　　　　　　　　Gabriel Fauré (1845–1924) Op. 23 No. 1

Background

Sully Prudhomme (1839–1907) won the Nobel Prize for literature in 1901 and was amongst the group of poets known as the Parnassians. Their style emphasised formal perfection and elegance, using classical or exotic subjects. This poem was set by Fauré in 1879. The famous rocking movement of the piano accompaniment evokes the gentle sway of the ships, and the song expresses both the longing for adventure and the heartache of those left back home.

Idiomatic translation

Along the quay, the great ships
that list silently in the swell
take no notice of the cradles
that the hands of the women rock.

But the day of farewells will come,
for it must be women who weep,
and that curious men explore
the horizons which lure them!

And on that day the great ships,
sailing off from the diminishing port,
feel their bulk held back
by the soul of the distant cradles.

Pronunciation – Les berceaux [lɛ bɛʀso]

Le long du quai, les grands vaisseaux,
lə lõ　dy ke　lɛ gʀɑ̃　vɛso

Que la　houle incline en silence,
kə　la ǀu(l)ɛ̃kli(n)ɑ̃　silɑ̃sə

Ne prennent pas garde aux berceaux
nə pʀɛnə　pa gaʀ(d)o　bɛʀso

Que la main des femmes balance.
kə la mɛ̃　dɛ famə　balɑ̃sə

Mais viendra le jour des adieux,
mɛ　vjɛ̃dʀa lə ʒuʀ dɛ(z)adjø

Car il faut que les femmes pleurent,
kaʀil fo　kə lɛ famə　plœʀə

Et que les hommes curieux
e kə lɛ(z)ɔmə　kyʀiø

Tentent les horizons qui leurrent!
tɑ̃tə　lɛ(z)ɔʀizõ　ki lœʀə

Et ce jour-là les grands vaisseaux,
e sə ʒuʀ la lɛ gʀɑ̃　vɛso

Fuyant le port qui diminue,
fɥijɑ̃　lə pɔʀ ki diminyə

Sentent leur masse retenue
sɑ̃tə　lœʀ masə ʀətənyə

Par l'âme des lointains berceaux.
paʀ lamə dɛ lwɛ̃tɛ̃　bɛʀso

Further notes

The final, neutral *e* in **diminue** and **retenue** should not be sung with too great an emphasis.

spoken text
piano accompaniment

Les berceaux
The cradles

Sully Prudhomme
(1839–1907)

Gabriel Fauré Op. 23 No. 1
(1845–1924)

Le long du quai,— les
The length of-the quay, the

grands— vais-seaux, Que la houle in-cline en si-len - ce,— Ne
large vessels, that the swell lists in silence, [do] not

pren - nent pas garde aux— ber-ceaux Que la main des fem - mes ba-
take notice of-the cradles that the hand of-the women ba-

-lan - - ce.— Mais vien-dra le
But will-come the

Prison

Prison　　　　　　　　　　　　　　　　　　　　Gabriel Fauré (1845–1924) Op. 83 No. 1

Background

Fauré and Verlaine met at the salon of Princess Edmond de Polignac (formerly Winnaretta Singer of the sewing-machine family) and thus began a productive artistic collaboration, with Fauré setting many of Verlaine's poems. 'Prison' describes Verlaine's own experience of imprisonment (after his attempted murder of the poet Arthur Rimbaud, the man he left his wife for) and Fauré's dramatic realisation is considered one of his most eloquent settings. Composed in 1894, it was published in 1896.

Idiomatic translation

The sky, above the roof,
Is so blue, so calm,
A tree, above the roof,
Rocks its leafy crown.

The bell, in the sky that one sees,
Sweetly rings,
A bird, on the tree that one sees,
Plaintively sings.

My God, my God, life is there,
Simple and tranquil!
That peaceful murmur there
Comes from the town.

What have you done, o you who are there,
Weeping unceasingly,
Say, what have you done, you who are there,
With your youth?

Pronunciation – **Prison** [prizõ]

Le ciel‿est, pardessus le toit,
lə sjɛlɛ　pardəsy lə twa

Si bleu, si calme,
si blø　si kalmə

Un‿arbre, pardessus le toit,
œ̃(n)arbrə pardəsy　lə twa

Berce sa palme.
bɛrsə sa palmə

La cloche dans le ciel qu'on voit,
la klɔʃə dɑ̃　lə sjɛl kõ　vwa

Doucement tinte,
dusəmɑ̃　tɛ̃tə

Un‿oiseau sur l'arbre qu'on voit,
œ̃(n)wazo syr larbrə kõ　vwa

Chante sa plainte.
ʃɑ̃tə　sa plɛ̃tə

Mon Dieu, mon Dieu la vie est là,
mõ　djø　mõ　djø　la vi ɛ　la

Simple‿et tranquille!
sɛ̃ple　trɑ̃kilə

Cette paisible rumeur-là
sɛtə　pɛziblə rymœr la

Vient de la ville.
vjɛ̃　də la vilə

Qu'as-tu fait, | ô toi que voilà,
ka　ty fɛ　o twa kə vwala

Pleurant sans cesse,
plœrɑ̃　sɑ̃　sɛsə

Dis, qu'as-tu fait, toi que voilà,
di　ka　ty fɛ　twa kə vwala

De ta jeunesse?
də ta ʒœnesə

Further notes

Note the pronunciation of **ville** and **tranquille**: the final *l* is sounded.

Prison
Prison

CD2 [5] *spoken text* [6] *piano accompaniment*

Paul Verlaine
(1844–96)

Gabriel Fauré Op. 83 No. 1
(1845–1924)

Le ciel est, par-des-sus le toit, Si bleu, si cal - me,
The sky is, above the roof, so blue, so calm,

Un ar-bre, par-des-sus le toit, Ber - ce sa pal - me.
a tree, above the roof, rocks its palm-leaf.

La clo-che dans le ciel qu'on voit, Dou-ce-ment tin - te,
The bell in the sky that one sees, softly rings,

Un oi-seau sur l'ar-bre qu'on voit, Chan-te sa plain - te. Mon
a bird on the tree that one sees, sings its plaint. My

Dieu, mon Dieu la vie est là, Sim - ple et tran - quil - le!
God, my God the life is there, simple and tranquil!

Cet - te pai - si - ble ru-meur-là Vient de la vil - le.
This peaceful murmur–there comes from the town.

Qu'as-tu fait, ô toi que voi-là, Pleu-rant sans ces - se,
What have you done, o you who (are) there, weeping without ceasing,

Dis, qu'as-tu fait, toi que voi-là,
say, what have you done, you who (are) there,

De ta jeu-nes - se?
with your youth?

La grotte

The grotto

Claude Debussy (1862–1918)

from *Trois chansons de France* No. 2

Background

Claude Debussy, born into a middle class family in St Germain-en-Laye, was one of the most influential composers of the 20th century. He was considered something of an outsider in the French musical tradition with his radical harmonies, and yet his music helped to define the musical aesthetic of the *fin-de-siècle* period. He composed in several genres, becoming the towering figure in the field of French song, but also wrote piano music (*Pour le piano, L'isle joyeuse*), orchestral pieces (*Ibéria, La mer*) and opera (*Pelléas et Mélisande*). Debussy began life as a promising pianist under the tutelage of Verlaine's mother-in-law, and to earn a living he played for singing lessons at the classes of Mme Moreau-Sainti where he was to develop a fascination for the singing voice. In 1904, the year that he wrote this song, both his mistress Gabrielle Dupont and his abandoned wife Lily had tried to commit suicide. Debussy had begun an affair with Emma Bardac, Fauré's former mistress, and the resulting scandal left him ostracized from the Parisian musical world. In his retreat, Debussy's songs became perhaps less accessible, but this song is wonderfully illustrative of his mature operatic style.

Idiomatic translation

Close to this dark grotto
Where one breathes such sweet air,
The water struggles with the pebbles
And the light with the shade.

These ripples, weary of the exercise
That they have made over the gravel,
Rest in this pool
Where once Narcissus died ...

The shadow of this vermillion flower
And of those bending rushes
Seem to be there within
The dreams of the sleeping water ...

Pronunciation – **La grotte** [la gʀɔt]

Auprès de cette grotte sombre
opʀɛ   də sɛtə gʀɔtə sõbʀə

Ces flots, lassés de l'exercice
sɛ   flo   lase   də lɛgsɛʀsisə

Où l'on respire un air si doux,
u   lõ   ʀɛspi(ʀ)œ(n)ɛʀ si du

Qu'ils ont fait dessus ce gravier,
kil(z)õ   fɛ   dəsy sə gʀavje

L'onde lutte avec les cailloux,
lõdə   lytavɛk   lɛ kaju

Se reposent dans ce vivier
sə ʀəpozə dã   sə vivje

Et la lumière avecque l'ombre.
e la lymjɛ(ʀ)avɛkə   lõbʀə

Où mourût | autrefois Narcisse ...
u   muʀy   otʀəfwa naʀsisə

L'ombre de cette fleur vermeille
lõbʀə   də sɛtə flœʀ vɛʀmejə

Et celle de ces joncs pendants
e sɛlə də sɛ ʒõ   pãdã

Paraissent estre là-dedans
paʀɛsə(t)ɛtʀə   la dədã

Les songes de l'eau qui sommeille ...
lɛ sõʒə də lo ki sɔmejə

Further notes

In the word **joncs** the *c* is not pronounced. In **estre** the *s* is not pronounced: it is an archaic form of **être**.

CD2 spoken text
piano accompaniment

La grotte
The grotto

Tristan L'Hermite François
(1601–55)

Claude Debussy
(1862–1918)

Très lent et très doux *(very slow and very soft)* [♩ = 36]

Original key

Au - près de cet - te grot - te som - bre Où l'on res - pi - re un
Close–by of this grotto dark where one breathes an

air si doux, L'on - de lutte a - vec les cail - loux, Et la lu -
air so sweet, the wave struggles with the pebbles, and the light

Testament

Testament   Henri Duparc (1848–1933)

Background

Henri Duparc was born in Paris and studied piano under César Franck at the Jesuit College of Vaugirard. His great reputation as a composer of French Mélodie rests on some sixteen surviving solo songs, written between the ages of 20 and 37. He lived until he was 85 but tragically, due to a mysterious nervous illness, wrote nothing for the rest of his life, and was so critical of what he had written that much was destroyed. Set to a text by the Symbolist poet Armand Silvestre, 'Testament' was written between 1883 and 1885 and dedicated to Madame Henri de Lassus.

Idiomatic translation

So that the wind may bear them to you
On the black wing of remorse,
I will write on the dead leaf
The tortures of my dead heart!

All my vigour has dried up
In the bright noons of your beauty,
And, like a withered leaf,
Nothing of life is left in me;

Your eyes have scorched me to the soul,
Like merciless suns!
A leaf that the abyss reclaims,
The south wind will carry me away too …

But before, so that it may bear them to you
On the black wing of remorse,
I will write on the dead leaf
The tortures of my dead heart!

Pronunciation – Testament [tɛstamã]

Pour que le vent te les apporte
puʀ kə lə vã tə lɛ(z)apɔʀtə

Sur l'aile noire   d'un remord,
syʀ lɛlə nwaʀə dœ̃ ʀəmɔʀ

J'écrirai sur la feuille morte
ʒekʀiʀe syʀ la fœjə mɔʀtə

Les tortures de mon coeur mort!
lɛ tɔʀtyʀə də mõ kœʀ mɔʀ

Toute ma sève s'est tarie
tutə ma sɛvə sɛ taʀiə

Aux clairs midis de ta beauté,
o klɛʀ midi də ta bote

Et, comme à la feuille flétrie,
e kɔ(m)a la fœjə fletʀiə

Rien de vivant ne m'est resté;
ʀjɛ̃ də vivã nə mɛ ʀɛste

Tes yeux m'ont brûlé jusqu'à l'âme,
tɛ(z)jø mõ bʀylə ʒyska lamə

Comme des soleils sans merci!
kɔmə de sɔlɛj sã mɛʀsi

Feuille que le gouffre réclame,
fœjə kə lə gufʀə ʀeklamə

L'autan va m'emporter aussi …
lotã va mãpɔʀte(ʀ)osi

Mais avant, pour qu'il te les porte
mɛ(z)avã puʀ kil tə lɛ pɔʀtə

Sur l'aile noire   d'un remord,
syʀ lɛlə nwaʀə dœ̃ ʀəmɔʀ

J'écrirai sur la feuille morte
ʒekʀiʀe syʀ la fœjə mɔʀtə

Les tortures de mon coeur mort!
lɛ tɔʀtyʀə də mõ kœʀ mɔʀ

Further notes

The final, neutral *es* in **tarie** and **flétrie** should be sung without too great an emphasis.

CD2 [9] spoken text
[10] piano accompaniment

Testament

Testament

Armand Silvestre
(1837–1901)

Henri Duparc
(1848–1933)

Mouvement modéré mais sans lenteur
(moderate movement but not slow) [♩. = 69]

marquez le chant *(emphasise the melody)*

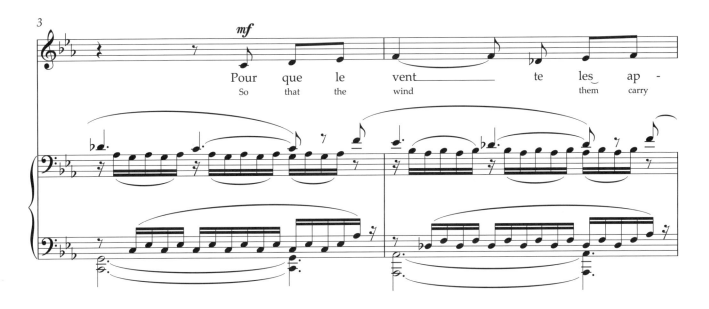

Pour que le vent___ te les ap-
So that the the wind them carry

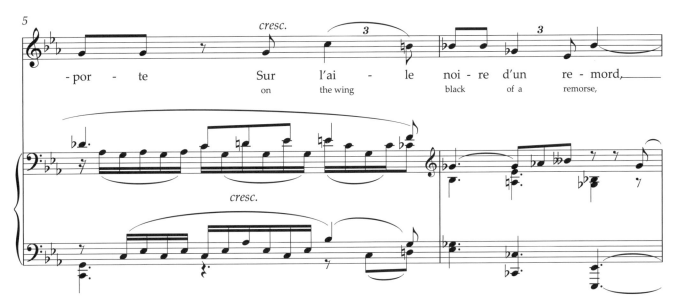

-por - te Sur l'ai - le noi - re d'un re - mord,___
on the wing black of a remorse,

Un peu plus lent (*a little slower*)

Tou - te ma sè - ve s'est ta -
All my sap is dried (up)

-ri - - - - - e Aux clairs mi -
in–the clear middays

poco rit.   a tempo

rall.

-ter aus - si...
also...

dim. molto

mf

poco rall.

dim.

mf

Tempo primo

mf

Mais _ a -
But   before,

-vant,   pour qu'il te les por - te   Sur l'ai - le noi - re d'un re - mord,_
so   that it you them carries   on   the wing black of a remorse,

cresc.

dim.

Chanson romanesque

Romantic song
from *Don Quichotte à Dulcinée*, No. 1

Maurice Ravel (1875–1937)

Background

Ravel was born near Biarritz and studied at the Paris Conservatoire, learning piano and composition under the guidance of Fauré. He wrote orchestral music – most famously perhaps the 'Boléro' (1928) – as well as ballet music, including *Daphnis et Chloé* (1909–12), piano music and thirty-nine songs, some of which, such as 'Shéhérazade' (1903), were orchestrated. In 1932, he received a head injury following an incident in a taxi. He began to suffer symptoms of aphasia (a disorder of the brain) and the set of three songs *Don Quichotte à Dulcinée* was his last work before he was unable to compose any longer. He finally died in 1937 having agreed to undergo a brain operation which was unsuccessful. The French text by Paul Morand is based on Cervantes' humorous, picaresque novel about an ageing Spanish gentlemen who, full of fantastical and idealistic notions of himself as a knight errant, sets off on an adventure with his squire, Sancho Panza, in love with the imaginary Dulcinea. This song is based on a Spanish dance known as a *guajira*.

Idiomatic translation

If you were to say that the earth
Offended you with so much turning,
I would dispatch Panza:
You would see it still and silent.

If you were to say that you are bored
By a sky too peopled with stars,
I would tear the divine order apart,
I would cut them down with one swipe.

If you were to say that space
Thus emptied, does not please you,
As a god-like knight, with a lance in his hand,
I would stud the fleeting wind with stars.

But were you to say that my blood
Is more mine than yours, my Lady,
I would pale beneath the rebuke
And I would die, blessing you.

O Dulcinea.

Pronunciation – Chanson romanesque [ʃɑ̃sõ ʀɔmanɛsk]

Si vous me disiez que la terre
si vu   mə dizje kə la tɛʀə

À tant tourner vous‿offensa,
a tɑ̃   tuʀne vu(z)ɔfɑ̃sa

Je lui dépêcherais Pança:
ʒə lɥi depeʃəʀɛ   pɑ̃sa

Vous la verriez fixe‿et se taire.
vu   la vɛʀje fikse sə tɛʀə

Si vous me disiez que l'ennui
si vu   me dizje kə lɑ̃nɥi

Vous vient du ciel trop fleuri d'astres,
vu   vjɛ̃   dy sjɛl tʀo flœri dastʀə

Déchirant les divins cadastres,
deʃiʀɑ̃   le divɛ̃   kadastʀə

Je faucherais d'un coup la nuit.
ʒə foʃəʀɛ   dœ̃ ku   la nɥi

Si vous me disiez que l'espace
si vu   mə dizje kə   lɛspasə

Ainsi vidé ne vous plaît point,
ɛ̃si   vide nə vu   plɛ   pwɛ̃

Chevalier Dieu, la lance‿au poing,
ʃəvalje   djø   la lɑ̃so   pwɛ̃

J'étoilerais le vent qui passe.
ʒetwaləʀɛ   lə vɑ̃   ki   pasə

Mais si vous disiez que mon sang
mɛ   si vu   dizje kə   mõ   sɑ̃

Est plus‿à moi qu'à vous, ma Dame,
ɛ   ply(z)a mwa ka   vu   ma damə

Je blêmirais dessous le blâme
ʒə blɛmiʀɛ   dəsu   lə blamə

Et je mourrais, vous bénissant.
e ʒə muʀɛ   vu   benisɑ̃

Ô Dulcinée.
o dylsineə

Further notes

Check the pronunciation of the characters' names in this song.

CD2  spoken text

piano accompaniment

Chanson romanesque
Romantic song

Paul Morand
(1888–1976)

Maurice Ravel
(1875–1937)

Si vous me di-siez que l'es - pa - ce Ain-si vi-dé - ne
If you me would–say that the space thus emptied not

vous plaît point, Che-va-lier Dieu, la lance au poing, J'é -
you pleased not, Knight God, the lance in–the fist, I

-toi-le-rais le vent qui pas - se.
would–stud (with stars) the wind who passes.

Mais si vous di-siez que mon sang Est plus à moi qu'à vous, ma
But if you would–say that my blood is more to me than to you, my

Нет, только тот, кто знал

None but the lonely heart   Pyotr Ilyich Tchaikovsky (1840–1893) Op. 6 No. 6

Background

Tchaikovsky, the son of a mining engineer and a mother of French ancestry, was born in the small town of Votkinsk. Being sent away to boarding school in St Petersburg at the age of ten, coupled with the sudden death of his beloved mother four years later, contributed to Tchaikovsky's sensitive and melancholic personality. Relationships with women were often idealised and it is widely believed that his struggles with homosexuality were to affect his life and music profoundly. In 1862 he began studying music under Zaremba at the St Petersburg Conservatory and went on to become a prolific composer, writing in many musical genres, including opera (*Queen of Spades* 1890 and *Eugene Onegin* 1878), orchestral music (six symphonies, *Romeo and Juliet* 1869–80, *1812 Overture* 1880), concertos for violin and piano, and ballet music (*Swan Lake* 1876 and *The Nutcracker* 1892). He also wrote over one hundred songs, and was commonly drawn to the theme of love and its loss. This popular song, written in 1869, uses the translation of Goethe's text *Nur wer die sehnsucht kennt* ('None but the lonely know'). It is one of the *Mignon* songs from *Wilhelm Meister* – the story of a young girl with a tragic past, rescued by Wilhelm from a travelling circus – and has come to represent the Romantic expression of the nostalgic search for a better and nobler world.

Idiomatic translation

Only one who has longed for a meeting (with a loved one)
can understand how I suffered and how I am still suffering.
I look into the distance ... I have no strength, my eyes grow dim ...
He who knew and loved me is far away!
Only one who has longed for a meeting (with a loved one)
can understand how I suffered and how I am still suffering.
My breast is burning ...
Only one who has longed for a meeting (with a loved one)
can understand how I suffered and how I am still suffering.

Pronunciation – **Нет, только тот, кто знал** [njɛt tɔljka tɔt ktɔ znɑl]

Нет, то́лько тот, кто знал
njɛt tɔljka   tɔt   ktɔ znɑl

свида́нья жа́жду,
svjidɑnja   ʒɑʒdu

поймёт, как я страда́л
pɑimjɔt   kɑk jɑ strɑdɑl

и как я стра́жду.
i   kɑk jɑ strɑʒdu

Гляжу́ я   вдаль ... нет сил,
gljɪʒu   jɑ vdɑlj.... njɛt sjil

тускне́ет око ...
tusknjɛjɪt   ɔkɑ

Ах, кто меня́   люби́л
ɑx   ktɔ mjɪnjɑ ljubjɪl

и знал далёко!
i   znɑl   dɑljɔkɑ

Вся грудь гори́т ...
fsjɑ grudj gɑrjɪt

CD2 🔘13 *spoken text*
🔘14 *piano accompaniment*

Нет, только тот, кто знал
None but the lonely heart

Lev Aleksandrovich Mey
(1822–62)

Pyotr Ilyich Tchaikovsky Op. 6 No. 6
(1840–93)

Andante non tanto [♩ = 72]

Original key
E♭ major

© 2008 by Faber Music Ltd

Средь шумного бала

At the ball　　　　　　　　　　　　Pyotr Ilyich Tchaikovsky (1840–93) Op. 38 No. 3

Background

In 1878, following the break-up of his disastrous marriage to Antonina Milyukova and the near completion of his opera *Eugene Onegin*, Tchaikovsky travelled to Europe, generously supported by his benefactress and confidante Nadezhda von Meck, and wrote a set of six Romances. Such songs would have been written for the private drawing-room and were settings of translations and contemporary Russian writers, in this case Count Alexei Tolstoy, who was a distant relative of the great Russian writer Leo Tolstoy. Alexei Tolstoy worked at court in St Petersburg as Grand Master of Royal Hunting, and upon retiring from service devoted his time to writing poetry, novels and plays.

Idiomatic translation

Amidst the noisy, whirling
bustle of the ball,
I saw you by chance,
but mystery enveloped your features.

Only your eyes looked sad,
and your wonderful voice
sounded like distant pipes,
like the playful waves of the sea.

Your slim waist entranced me,
your pensive look
and your laugh, both sad and ringing,
since then, has echoed in my heart.

Weary, in the lonely hours of the night,
I like to lie down.
I see your sad eyes,
hear your happy words ...

And sorrowfully drifting
into slumber and unknown dreams,
I wonder whether I love you,
but it seems to me that I do!

Pronunciation – **Средь шумного бала, случайно** [sɾjɛdj ʃumnava bɑla slutʃɑina]

Средь шу́много ба́ла, случа́йно,
sɾjɛdj ʃumnava bɑla slutʃɑina

В трево́ге мирско́й суеты́,
ftɾjivɔgjɛ mjirskɔi sujɪtɨ

Тебя́ я уви́дел, но та́йна
tjɪbjɑ ja uvjɪdjɪl nɔ tɑina

Твой покрыва́ла черты́.
tvɑi pakɾivɑla tʃirtɨ

Лишь о́чи печа́льно гляде́лн,
ljiʃ ɔtʃi pjɪtʃɑljna gljɪdjɛlji

А го́лос так ди́вно звуча́л,
a gɔlas tak djivna zvutʃɑl

Как звон отдале́нной свире́ли,
kɑk zvɔn ad:daljɔnːnai svjirjɛlji

Как мо́ря игра́юший вал.
kɑk mɔrja igrɑjuʃtʃi val

Мне стан твой понра́вился то́нкий,
mnjɛ stan tvɔi panrɑvjilsa tɔnkji

И весь твой заду́мчивый вид,
i vjɛsj tvɔi zadumtʃivɪ vjit

А смех твой, и гру́стный, и зво́нкий,
a smjɛx tvɔi i grusnɪ i zvɔnkji

С тех пор в моём се́рдце звучи́т.
stjɛx pɔr vmajɔm sjɛrtsɛ zvutʃit

В часы́ одино́кие но́чи
ftʃasɨ adjinɔkjija nɔtʃi

Люблю́ я, уста́лый, приле́чь;
ljublju ja ustalɪ pɾiljɛtʃ

Я ви́жу печа́льные о́чи,
ja vjiʒu pjɪtʃɑljnɪje ɔtʃi

Я слы́шу весёлую речь,
ja slɨʃu vjisjɔluju rjɛtʃ

И гру́стно я, гру́стно так засыпа́ю,
i grusna ja grusna tak zasɨpɑju

И в грёзах неве́домых сплю ...
i vgɾjɔzax njɛvjɛdamɨx splju

Люблю́ ли тебя́, я не зна́ю,
ljublju lji tjɪbjɑ ja njɛ znɑju

Но ка́жется мне, что люблю́!
nɔ kaʒɛtsa mnjɛ ʃtɔ ljublju

CD2 15 *spoken text*
16 *piano accompaniment*

Средь шумного бала
At the ball

Alexei Tolstoy
(1817–75)

Pyotr Ilyich Tchaikovsky Op. 38 No. 3
(1840–93)

114

Не верь, мой друг

Believe it not, my friend   Pyotr Ilyich Tchaikovsky (1840–93) Op. 6 No. 1

Background

This song comes from Tchaikovsky's first set of six Romances written in 1869. Such songs would have been written for the private drawing-room and were settings of translations and of contemporary Russian writers, in this case Count Alexei Tolstoy, who was a distant relative of the great Russian writer Leo Tolstoy. Alexei Tolstoy worked at court in St Petersburg as Grand Master of Royal Hunting, and upon retiring from service devoted his time to writing poetry, novels and plays.

Idiomatic translation

Do not believe, my friend, when in an outburst of grief
I say I have ceased to love you!
At the hour of the ebb tide, do not believe that the sea is unfaithful,
It will lovingly come back to land.

I'm already yearning, full of the same old passion,
I will give my freedom to you again,
And already, the roaring waves are running back
From afar to the beloved shores.

Pronunciation – **Не верь, мой друг** [njɛ vjɛrj mɔi druk]

Не верь, мой друг, когда́ в поры́ве го́ря
njɛ vjɛrj mɔi druk kagdɑ fparɨvjɛ gɔrja

Я говорю́, что разлюби́л тебя́,
ja gavarju ʃtɔ razljubjil tjɪbja

В отли́ва час не верь, изме́не мо́ря,
vatljiva tʃas njɛ vjɛrj izmjɛnjɛ mɔrja

Оно́ к земле́ воро́тится любя́.
anɔ kzjimljɛ varɔtjitsa ljubja

Уж я тоску́ю, пре́жней стра́сти по́лный,
uʃ ja taskuju prjɛʒnjɛi strɑstji pɔlnɨ

Свою́ свобо́ду вновь тебе́ отда́м
svaju svabɔdu vnɔfj tjɪbjɛ ad:dɑm

И уж бегу́т обра́тно с шу́мом во́лны
i uʃ bjigut abrɑtna ʃʃumam vɔlnɨ

Издалека́ к люби́мым берега́м.
izdaljɪkɑ kljubjimɨm bjɪrjɪgɑm

CD2 spoken text / piano accompaniment

Не верь, мой друг

Believe it not, my friend

Alexei Tolstoy
(1817–75)

Pyotr Ilyich Tchaikovsky Op. 6 No. 1
(1840–93)

*Recording cue

Нам звёзды кроткие сияли

The stars looked tenderly upon us   Pyotr Ilyich Tchaikovsky (1840–93) Op. 60 No. 12

Background

By August 1886, Tchaikovsky was living in Maidanovo and working on a new opera entitled *The Enchantress*. As ever, he was struggling with bouts of depression and a waning creative drive, but the arrival of some friends, and a particular request from the Empress Maria Fyodorovna to dedicate a romance to her, led to a burst of composition and ten of the final twelve Romances of Opus 60 were written. The Empress was apparently delighted with his gift of the set and responded in turn by sending him a signed portrait. The text by Alexei Pleshcheyev is on a familiar theme of Tchaikovsky's: the loss of love through the forces of fate or destiny. Pleshcheyev was a translator and one of the exponents of 19th century Russian 'civic poetry' – a movement that was concerned to express the politics and social conditions of ordinary peasant people. He had known Tchaikovsky in Moscow and the composer had earlier set the poet's collection of children's poems *The Snowdrop* to music in his Op. 54 *Children's Songs*.

Idiomatic translation

The stars gently shone for us,
A slight breeze was softly blowing,
Fragrant flowers were around us,
And waves sweetly murmured
At our feet.

We were young, we loved,
And gazed into the distance with trust;
Optimistic dreams dwelled within us,
And for us, the blizzards of grey winter
Were not frightening.

Where are those radiant nights
With their fragrant beauty
And mysterious murmuring waves,
Enthusiastic hopes and visions,
Where is that bright multitude?

The stars have faded, and the
Pale flowers have wilted …
When will you forget, oh heart,
Everything that used to be,
All that Spring gave us?

Pronunciation – **Нам звёзды кроткие сияли** [nɑm zvjɔzdɨ krɔtkjijɛ sjijɑlji]

Нам звёзды кро́ткие сия́ли,
nɑm zvjɔzdɨ krɔtkjijɛ sjijɑlji

Чуть ве́ял ти́хий ветеро́к,
tʃutj vjɛjal tjixji vjɪtjɪrɔk

Круго́м цветы́ благоуха́ли,
krugɔm tsvjɪtɨ blagauxɑlji

И во́лны ла́сково журча́ли
i vɔlnɨ lɑskava ʒurtʃɑlji

У на́ших ног.
u nɑʃɪx nɔk

Мы бы́ли ю́ны, мы люби́ли,
mɨ bɨlji junɨ mɨ ljubjɪlji

И с мело в даль смотре́ли мы;
i smjɛla vdalj smatrjɛlji mɨ

В нас грёзы ра́дужные жи́ли,
vnas grjɔzɨ rɑduʒnɨjɛ ʒɨlji

И нам не стра́шны вьюги бы́ли
i nɑm nji straʃnɨ vjugji bɨlji

Седо́й зимы́.
sjidɔi zjimɨ

Где ж э́ти но́чи с их сия́ньем,
gdjeʒ ɛtji nɔtʃi six sjijɑnjim

С благоуха́ющей красо́й
sblagauxɑjuʃtʃɛi krasɔi

И волн таи́нственным журча́ньем,
i vɔln tainstvjin:nɨm ʒurtʃɑnjim

Наде́жд, восто́рженных мечта́ний,
nadjɛʒt vastɔrʒɛn:nɨx mjɪtʃtɑnji

Где све́тлый рой?
gdjɛ svjɛtlɨ rɔi

Поме́ркли звёзды, и уны́ло
pamjɛrklji zvjɔzdɨ i unɨla

Пони́кли бле́клые цветы́ …
panjiklji blɛklɨjɛ tsvjɪtɨ

Когда́ ж, о се́рдце, всё, что бы́ло,
kagdɑʃ ɔ sjɛrtsɛ fsjɔ ʃtɔ bɨla

Что нам весна́ с тобо́й дари́ла,
ʃtɔ nɑm vjɪsnɑ stabɔi darjɪla

Забу́дешь ты?
zabudjɪʃ tɨ

Нам звёзды кроткие сияли

The stars looked tenderly upon us

Alexei Pleshcheyev
(1825–93)

Pyotr Ilyich Tchaikovsky Op. 60 No. 12
(1840–93)

© 2008 by Faber Music Ltd

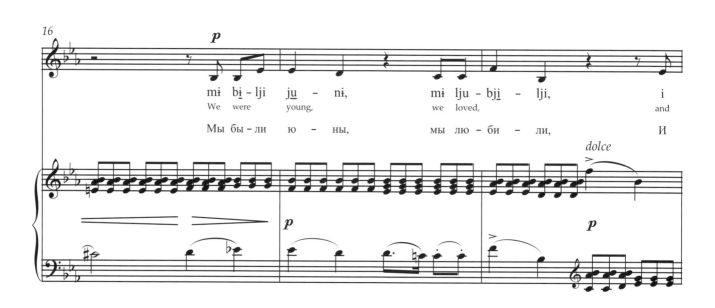

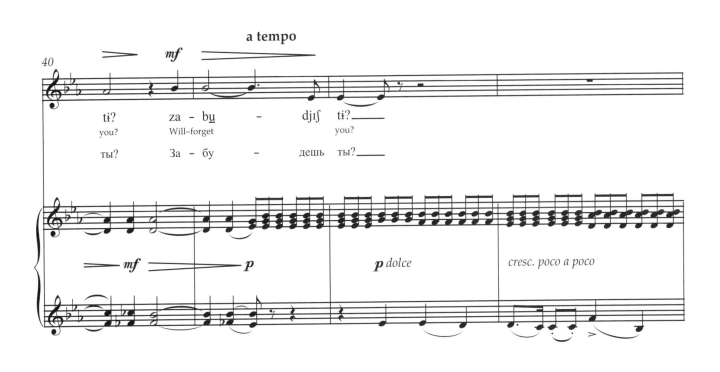

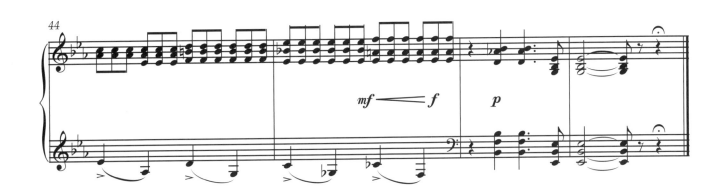

Key to International Phonetic Alphabet for Italian

Vowels	IPA	English sounds	Italian words
A	[a]	as in a bright 'ah'	caro [karɔ]
E	[ɛ]	open as in 'b<u>e</u>d'	bella [bɛl:la]
	[e]	close (prepare your tongue as if to say 'ee' and say 'ay' without dropping the jaw)	che [ke]
I	[i]	as in 's<u>ee</u>' or 'pol<u>i</u>ce'	mi [mi], ti [ti]
O	[o]	close (say 'oh' with lips in a well-rounded position, jaw slightly dropped and no diphthong)	dolce [doltʃe]
	[ɔ]	open as in 'h<u>o</u>t'	bocca [bɔk:ka]
U	[u]	as in 'f<u>oo</u>d' or 'r<u>u</u>de'	tu [tu]

(Check the pronunciation guides carefully for open and closed vowels as Italian spelling does not differentiate these sounds.)
Note: There are no diphthongs in Italian – the vowels are often liaised but nevertheless are clearly delineated.

Semi-vowels

[j]	as in '<u>y</u>ard'		piacer [pjatʃer]
[w]	as in '<u>w</u>ater'		acqua [ak:kwa]

Consonants

B, F, M and V are pronounced as in English.
D, N, T and L are pronounced as in English but with the tip of the tongue in a forward position, just behind the upper front teeth.

C	[tʃ]	as in '<u>ch</u>urch'	*before e or i*	ciel [tʃel], dicesti [ditʃesti]
C	[k]	as in '<u>c</u>ook'	*before a, o or u*	cor [kɔr]
SC	[ʃ]	as in '<u>sh</u>oe'	*before e or i*	scena [ʃena]
SC	[sk]	as in '<u>sk</u>ull'		schiudi [skjudi], scherzo [skertsɔ]
G	[dʒ]	as in '<u>j</u>ar'	*before e or i*	giro [dʒirɔ], dipinge [dipindʒe]
G	[g]	as in '<u>g</u>ood'		largo [largɔ], goder [goder]
P	[p]	as in '<u>p</u>ull'		pace [patʃe]
QU	[kw]	as in '<u>qu</u>ick'		quel [kwel]
R	[ɾ]	slightly flipped 'r'	*between two vowels*	caro [karɔ]
R	[r]	trilled/rolled 'r'		ritardando [ritardandɔ]
S	[s]	as in '<u>s</u>o'		subito [subitɔ]
S	[z]	as in '<u>z</u>oo'		rosa [rozа]
Z	[ts]	as in 'pe<u>ts</u>'		grazia [grat:tsja], sembianze [sembjantse]
Z	[dz]	as in 'a<u>dds</u>'		mezzo [med:dzɔ]

Extra notes

-GLI-	[ʎ]	like 'mi<u>lli</u>on'	*(the g is silent)*	voglio [vɔʎɔ]
-GN-	[ɲ]	like '<u>n</u>ew' (ny-oo)	*(the g is silent)*	segno [seɲɔ]
-NG-	[ng]	Try to avoid the English 'ng' sound as in 'bri<u>ng</u>'. When singing, the 'n' may still be formed as above.		vengo [vengɔ]
H		is always silent		hanno [an:nɔ]
H		hardens C, G and SC		chi [ki], schiudi [skjudi]
I		is silent when used to soften C, G, or SC		già [dʒa], lascia [laʃa]

Double consonants

All double consonants should be emphasized with a slight 'stop' of the vowel before them – as in oggetto [ɔd:ʒet:tɔ], mattinata [mat:tinata].
A single r is lightly flipped. A double rr is strongly rolled.

Word endings

When singing in Italian, final vowels (unless marked with an accent eg: più [pju]) should never be stressed.

Key to International Phonetic Alphabet for German

Vowels	IPA	English sounds	German words
A	[aː]	long – as in 'far'	Vater [faːtə]
	[a]	short – as in 'undo'	Mann [man]
E	[eː]	long – no direct English equivalent but exactly the same as French é (prepare your tongue as if to say 'ee' and say 'ay' without dropping the jaw)	lebe [leːbə]
	[ɛ]	short – as in 'bed' or 'set'	denn [dɛn]
	[ə]	neutral – as in 'the' or 'again'	deine [dainə]
I	[iː]	long – as in 'see' or 'police'	die [diː], ihm [ǀiːm]
	[ɪ]	short – as in 'sit' or 'bin'	im [ǀɪm], ich [ǀɪç]
O	[oː]	long (say 'oh' with lips almost as closed as if for 'ooh' and with no diphthong)	Wohnung [voːnʊŋ]
	[ɔ]	short – as in 'hot'	kommt [kɔmt]
U	[uː]	long – as in 'food' or 'rude'	du [duː], Ruh [ruː]
	[ʊ]	short – as in 'put' or 'book'	und [ǀʊnt], um [ǀʊm]

Modified vowels

ä	[ɛː]	long – as in 'gate'	Tränen [trɛːnən]
	[ɛ]	short – as in 'bed' or 'set'	Hände [hɛndə]
ö	[œ]	short – the same sound as 'earth' but shorter	Hölle [hœlə]
	[øː]	long – as above but with lips more closed (the same as French 'deux')	schöne [ʃøːnə]
ü	[yː]	long (say 'ee' with closed lips in an 'oo' shape)	über [yːbɐ], Frühling [fryːlɪŋ]
	[ʏ]	short (try saying 'it' with closed lips in an 'oo' shape)	drücket [drʏkət]

Dipthongs

ai, ei	[ai]	as in 'aisle' or 'height'	Mai [mai], mein [main]
au	[au]	as in 'house' or 'flower'	Auge [ǀaugə], Frau [frau]
äu, eu	[ɔi]	as in 'boy' or 'oil'	Äuglein [ǀɔiglain], neu [nɔi]

As in English, when singing a diphthong, spend most time on the first of the combined vowels, leaving the second to the last moment before finishing the word or syllable.

Glottal stop [ǀ]

The slight stopping of the breath and starting the sound (as in 'umbrella') takes place in German before any word beginning with a vowel. The intensity of this is open to artistic interpretation, but it should never be overdone or create any danger of injuring the voice.

Consonants

Consonants are pronounced as in English with the following exceptions:

g is always pronounced hard as in 'good' (*but see* 'Endings' *below*)	Glanz [glants]
h is silent after a vowel, otherwise it is aspirated	Sohn [zoːn] Herz [hɛrts]
j is pronounced as an English 'y' as in 'yes'	ja [jaː]
k is pronounced before 'n' (it is never silent)	Knabe [knaːbə]
r is slightly 'flipped' [ɾ] before a consonant	Herz [hɛrts], sterben [ʃtɛrbən]
r is rolled [r] at the beginning of word or after another consonant	Rose [roːzə] Grab [grap]
s before vowels, as in English 'z' (*but see below*)	sein [zain] Rose [roːzə]
v mostly as in English 'f'	voll [fɔl]
w as in English 'v'	wenn [vɛn]
z as in 'cats'	zum [tsʊm] Schmerz [ʃmɛrts]

Double consonants and other sounds

Vowels	IPA	English sounds	German words
ck	[k]	as in 'lock'	Blick [blɪk]
ch	[x]	after **a, o, u** and **au** – closest to Scottish 'loch' (place tongue in the position for 'k' and say 'h')	doch [dɔx], nach [nax]
ch	[ç]	after **e, i, ä, eu** or a consonant as in (whispered) 'yes' (place tongue in the position for 'ee' and say 'h')	ich [ǀɪç], durch [dʊrç]
ph	[f]	as in 'telephone'	Phantasie [fantazi:]
pf	[pf]	both letters sounded	Pforten [pfɔrtən]
qu	[kv]	sounds like English 'kv...'	Qual [kva:l]
ß	[s]	as in 'kiss'	laß [las]
sch	[ʃ]	as in English 'ship'	schöne [ʃø:nə]
sp, st	[ʃp, ʃt]	sounds like English 'sht' or 'shp' *(at the beginning of a word, or after a prefix)*	Spiel [ʃpi:l], still [ʃtɪl] erstanden [ǀɛɐʃtandən]
-ng	[ŋ]	as in 'sing'	kling [klɪŋ]

Note: Unlike Italian, where double consonants are marked, in German they are treated as single consonants unless the need to express the word more imaginatively leads to emphasizing them (this is equally true of single consonants).

Endings of words/prefixes/word elements

-er	[ɐ]	as in 'sister'	guter [gu:tɐ]
-r	[ɐ]	usually not pronounced (but check IPA in songs for exceptions)	nur [nu:ɐ], vor [fo:ɐ]
-en	[ən]	as in 'garden'	meinen [mainən]
b		at the end of a word sounds 'p'	Grab [grap]
d		at the end of a word sounds 't'	Lied [li:t], und [ǀʊnt]
s		at the end of a word as in 'less'	liebes [li:bəs], dies [di:s]
g		at the end of a word sounds 'k'	Sonntag [zɔnta:k]
-ig	[ɪç]	as in the German word 'ich'	ewig [ǀeviç]

General note

Even though there are many consonants in German, the legato line (as in all singing) is still paramount and consonants need to be quick and crisp.

Key to International Phonetic Alphabet for French

Vowels	IPA	English sounds	French words
a	[ɑ]	long – as in 'f<u>ar</u>'	âme [<u>ɑ</u>mə]
	[a]	short – as in a bright 'ah'	la, [l<u>a</u>], amour [amuʀ]
e	[e]	long (prepare your tongue as if to say 'ee' and say 'ay' without dropping the jaw)	été [et<u>e</u>], et [<u>e</u>]
	[ɛ]	short – as in 'b<u>e</u>d' or 's<u>e</u>t'	est [<u>ɛ</u>], belle [bɛlə]
	[ə]	neutral – as in 'th<u>e</u>'	le [l<u>ə</u>], que [k<u>ə</u>]
i	[i]	long – as in 's<u>ee</u>' or 'pol<u>i</u>ce'	si [s<u>i</u>], qui [k<u>i</u>]
o	[o]	long (say 'oh' with lips in a well-rounded position, jaw slightly dropped and no diphthong)	rose [ʀ<u>o</u>zə], vos [v<u>o</u>]
	[ɔ]	short – as in 'h<u>o</u>t'	comme [k<u>ɔ</u>mə]
u	[y]	long (say 'ee' with well-rounded lips in an 'oo' shape)	tu [t<u>y</u>], une [<u>y</u>nə]
ou	[u]	long – as in 'f<u>oo</u>d' or 'r<u>u</u>de'	tous [t<u>u</u>s], pour [p<u>u</u>ʀ]
eu	[œ]	open (say '<u>ear</u>th' and drop the jaw)	leur [l<u>œ</u>ʀ], cœur [k<u>œ</u>ʀ]
	[ø]	closed (as above but with lips well-rounded)	deux [d<u>ø</u>], feu [f<u>ø</u>]

Nasalized vowels

	[ɑ̃]	long [ɑ] (f<u>ar</u>) nasalized	blanc [bl<u>ɑ̃</u>], semble [s<u>ɑ̃</u>blə]
	[ɛ̃]	short [æ] (f<u>a</u>t) nasalized	matin [mat<u>ɛ̃</u>], essaim [es<u>ɛ̃</u>]
	[õ]	long [o] (<u>oh</u>) nasalized	mon [m<u>õ</u>], ombre [<u>õ</u>bʀə]
	[œ̃]	short [œ] (th<u>e</u>) nasalized	un [<u>œ̃</u>], parfum, [paʀf<u>œ̃</u>]

Although nasal vowels are always followed by an -n or -m in the spelling, these consonants are **not** pronounced either in speech or in singing unless they form a liaison with a word beginning with a vowel.

Semi-vowels

	[j]	using an English 'y' sound, as in 'p<u>i</u>ano'	bien [bj<u>ɛ̃</u>], ciel [sj<u>ɛ</u>l]
	[w]	as in 'q<u>u</u>ack'	moi [mwa], voyant [vw<u>a</u>jɑ̃]
	[ɥ]	Try to say the 'y' in 'une' very quickly before the 'i'. It should not sound like a 'w'.	lui [lɥ<u>i</u>], nuit [nɥ<u>i</u>]

Consonants

b d f k l m n p t v w y x z

The above consonants are pronounced as in English, though in French (as in Italian) there is no explosion of breath with **p, t, k**. Also, double consonants are not marked and are spoken or sung as if single.

c	[k]	hard as in 'cook'	*before a,o,u/ending words*	comme [k<u>ɔ</u>mə], lac [lak]
c/ç	[s]	soft as in 'piece'	*c-before e, i/ç- before a, u, o*	ce [sə], français [fʀɑ̃s<u>ɛ</u>]
g	[g]	hard as in 'good'	*before a, o, u*	gauche [goʃə]
	[ʒ]	soft as in 'plea<u>s</u>ure'	*before e, i*	age [aʒə]
h		is usually silent		hélas [|elas]
j	[ʒ]	is pronounced as in 'plea<u>s</u>ure'		je [ʒə], jardin [ʒaʀd<u>ɛ̃</u>]
l	[l]	like an Italian 'forward' 'l' (soft and quick) *(but also sometimes silent)*		lune [lynə], gentil [ʒɑ̃ti]
qu	[k]	pronounced as a 'k' and without the 'w'		que, [kə] qui [ki]
r	[ʀ]	uvula is vibrated by a vocalised breath against the back of the tongue (see note below)		rien [ʀi<u>ɛ̃</u>]
s	[s]	unvoiced as in 's<u>o</u>'		sur [syʀ]
	[z]	voiced as in 'ga<u>z</u>e'	*between two vowels*	rosée [roz<u>e</u>ə]
x	[ks]	as in 'e<u>x</u>ample'		extase [ɛkst<u>ɑ</u>zə]
	[gs]	as in 'e<u>gg</u>s'		examiner [ɛgzamine]
	[z]		*in a liaison*	deux amis [dø(z)ami]
		silent as a final consonant	*no liaison*	deux [dø], yeux [jø]

Other sounds

Vowels	IPA	English sounds		French words
-ai	[e]	closed 'e' at the end of a word		aimerai [ɛməʀe̠]
-ais/-ait/-aient	[ɛ]	open 'e' at the end of a word (verb endings)		mais [mɛ̠], avaient [avɛ̠]
-au/-eau	[o]	long (say 'oh' with lips in a well-rounded position, jaw slightly dropped and no diphthong)		beau [bo̠]
ch	[ʃ]	as in '<u>sh</u>oe'		chanter [ʃɑ̃te]
-ail	[aj]	as in English 'eye' (with a pronounced 'y')		travail [trava̠j]
-eil	[ɛj]	as in English 'eh' followed by 'y'		sommeil [sɔmɛ̠j]
-euil/oeil	[œj]	as in English 'err' followed by 'y'		feuille [fœj], oeil [œj]
-ouille	[uj]	as in English 'ooh' followed by 'y'		mouiller [muje̠]
-ille/quille	[ilə]	as in '<u>e</u>longate'		ville [vilə], tranquille [tʀɑ̃kilə]
-er/ez	[e]		*as a word ending*	monter [mɔ̃te̠], assez [ase̠]
-gn-	[ɲ]	as in 'o<u>n</u>ion'		ligne [liɲə]
ph	[f]	as in 'tele<u>ph</u>one'		séraphin [seʀafɛ̃]
th	[t]	pronounced as a 't'		théatre [tea̠tʀə]

Word endings

A final -e, -es and the verb ending -ent are silent in speech, but in singing are often given a note. These are sung to the neutral [ə] vowel but should never be emphasized; phrase them off tastefully wherever possible.

Liaisons

The decision whether or not to join the final consonant (or consonant plus [ə]) to a following word beginning with a vowel is always a thorny one and the academic rules are complex. Contemporary tastes are always evolving and liaisons are used increasingly less frequently. In this volume, the IPA liaisons should be executed gently and without too much emphasis.

Vocalic harmonisation

In French, vocalic harmonisation is the rhyming of closely related vowel sounds around adjoining syllables (either within one word or between two neighbouring words). It happens with only two pairs of vowels: between [ɛ] and [e] and between [ə] and [ø], and occurs when one of these open vowels is followed by its closed counterpart and the open vowel closes to rhyme with it. It does not work the other way round. Thus *baiser* [bɛze] and *cheveux* [ʃəvø] become [beze] and [ʃøvø], and *les étoiles* [lɛ(z)etwalə] becomes [lez(e)twalə]. This occurs in speech but cannot be assumed in every case in singing and is open to artistic interpretation. Check the IPA guide carefully for each song and listen to the CD for any suggested vocalic harmonisation.

Rolling the 'r' in French

In classical singing, it has been considered good taste to pronounce the rolled 'r' in the Italian style (i.e. with the tip of the tongue in a forward position). Contemporary tastes, however, seem to be moving towards the traditional uvular 'r', even in classical song and opera. In this guide, we recommend the uvular 'r' [ʀ]. In French Baroque repertoire, however, a rolled Italian 'r' [ɾ] would still be considered stylistic.

Key to International Phonetic Alphabet for Russian

Phonetics or transliteration

Note that in this edition and in keeping with the principles of *The Language of Song* series, we have used a phonetic system to show Russian sounds, rather than a transliteration. Therefore, some sounds are represented with different symbols. Study this simple key to familiarise yourself with the Russian sounds.

This system has been simplified to offer a basic pronunciation of the language. For a more comprehensive and thorough explanation of the rules of Russian pronunciation, see *Russian Songs and Arias* by Jean Piatak and Regina Avrashov (published 1991, Caldwell Publishing Co).

Vowels

There are 'hard' and 'soft' vowels and consonants in Russian. The vowel governs the preceding consonant. Therefore, if the vowel is 'soft', the preceding consonant will be correspondingly 'soft' and if the vowel is 'hard', the preceding consonant is 'hard'.

Vowels	IPA	English sounds		Russian words
(Hard)				
А а	[ɑ]	as in 'far'		как [kɑk], давно́ [dɑvnɔ]
Э э	[ɛ]	as in 'bed'		это [ɛta]
Ы ы	[ɨ]	prepare to say 'ü' [y:] but say 'ee' [i] in a guttural position		вы [vɨ]
О о	[ɔ]	as in 'hot'		вóпли [vɔplji]
У у	[u]	as in 'food' or 'rude'		скýчно [skuʃna]
(Soft)				
Я я	[jɑ]	as in 'yard'		явка [jɑfka]
Е е	[jɛ]	as in 'yes'		едет [jɛdɪt]
И и	[i]	as in 'see'		ива [iva]
Й й	[i]	as in 'toy'	*(the end of a diphthong)*	той [tɔi]
Ё ё	[jɔ]	as in 'yore'		ёлка [jɔlkɑ]
Ю ю	[ju]	as in 'you'		юность [junastj]

Note: In Russian, vowel pronunciation can change depending on the stress of words (marked above the Cyrillic letter with an accent [′]), or the consonants used.

О	can become [ɑ] *see above* or [a] as in 'undo'		собой [sabɔi], поля́х [paljɑx]
Е е	can become [ɛ] *see above* or [ɪ] as in 'sit'		цветок [tsvjɪtɔk]
Я я	can become [jɪ], or [ja]		ярова́ [jɪravɑ], явить [jɪvitj] горя [gɔrja]

There are three exceptions where the consonant governs the vowel. After **Ж, Ш** and **Ц**, the vowel is always hard; for example, in the word **жива́** [ʒivɑ], the **И** [i] is hardened to a [ɨ] sound. Listen to the CD and follow the phonetics carefully.

Consonants

In the chart below, the softening of the consonants is represented most closely by the 'y' [j] sound. This should, however, be executed very lightly, as a passing sound only.

	(hard)		(soft)			(hard)		(soft)	
Б б	[b]	body	[bj]	beauty	П п	[p]	pop	[pj]	pew
Д д	[d]	day	[dj]	dew	Р р	[r]	'rolled'	[rj]	'flipped' in
Ф ф	[f]	far	[fj]	few					'soft' position
Г г	[g]	game	[gj]	argue	С с	[s]	sad	[sj]	assume
К к	[k]	cat	[kj]	cue	Т т	[t]	talk	[tj]	costume
Л л	[l]	hull	[lj]	million *(or Ital. 'gli')*	В в	[v]	voice	[vj]	view
М м	[m]	man	[mj]	music	Х х	[x]	German 'ach'	[xj]	no equivalent
Н н	[n]	net	[nj]	new	З з	[z]	zoo	[zj]	resume

Double consonants

Double consonants in Russian are treated in a similar way to Italian double consonants. They are shown in phonetics by a lengthening symbol [ː] and should be emphasized by a slight 'stop' on the sound, e.g.: **отдаленной** [adːdaljɛnːnɑi].

Other sounds

Ж ж	(hard)	[ʒ]	as in 'plea<u>s</u>ure'	жар [ʒɑr]
Ц ц	(hard)	[ts]	as in 'ca<u>ts</u>' or '<u>ts</u>ar'	царь [tsɑrj]
Ч ч	(soft)	[tʃ]	as in '<u>ch</u>ur<u>ch</u>'	час [tʃas]
Ш ш	(hard)	[ʃ]	as in '<u>sh</u>oe'	шум [ʃum]
Щ щ	(soft)	[ʃtʃ]	as in 'pu<u>shch</u>air'	прощай [prɑʃtʃɑi]

The symbols Ъ and Ь

These symbols do not have sounds of their own but are very important in Russian spelling as they affect the sound of the preceding consonants.

Ъ ъ	hardens a preceding consonant	объятия [abjɑtjijɑ]
Ь ь	softens a preceding consonant	больной [baljnɔi]

Voiced and voiceless consonant sounds

Some voiced consonants can be pronounced as their voiceless equivalents. Final consonants are often voiceless. Be aware of the following consonant pairs but follow the phonetics and CD carefully.

voiced	voiceless
б [b]	**п** [p]
в [v]	**ф** [f]
г [g]	**к** [k]
д [d]	**т** [t]
ж [ʒ]	**ш** [ʃ]
з [z]	**с** [s]

New and Old Russian

In 1918, a new decree on orthography abolished the letters **i, ѣ** and **ѳ** in Russian and replaced them with **и, е** or (**ё**), and **ф**. In this edition, we have used the new Russian Cyrillic alphabet throughout.

Also available in the Language of Song series

ELEMENTARY
High Voice & Low Voice

ISBN10: 0-571-52345-5
ELEMENTARY HIGH

ISBN10: 0-571-52346-3
ELEMENTARY LOW

Contents

Caro mio ben • Tommaso Giordani

Santa Lucia • Teodoro Cottrau

Non lo dirò col labbro • Georg Frideric Handel

Sebben, crudele • Antonio Caldara

Nina • Anonymous

Alma del core • Antonio Caldara

Nel cor più non mi sento • Giovanni Paisiello

Vittoria, mio core! • Giacomo Carissimi

Gruß • Felix Mendelssohn

An die Laute • Franz Schubert

Kinderwacht • Robert Schumann

Frühlingslied • Franz Schubert

Wiegenlied • Johannes Brahms

Sonntag • Johannes Brahms

Heidenröslein • Franz Schubert

Dein blaues Auge • Johannes Brahms

Chevaliers de la table ronde • French folksong

Bois épais • Jean-Baptiste Lully

En prière • Gabriel Fauré

Lydia • Gabriel Fauré

INTERMEDIATE
High Voice & Low Voice

ISBN10: 0-571-52343-9
INTERMEDIATE HIGH

ISBN10: 0-571-52344-7
INTERMEDIATE LOW

Contents

Tu lo sai • Giuseppe Torelli

Toglietemi la vita ancor • Alessandro Scarlatti

Amarilli, mia bella • Giulio Caccini

Se tu m/ami • attr. Alessandro Parisotti

Vaga luna • Vincenzo Bellini

An Chloë • Wolfgang Amadeus Mozart

Vergebliches Ständchen • Johannes Brahms

Ständchen • Franz Schubert

Mariä Wiegenlied • Max Reger

Die Lotosblume • Robert Schumann

Die Forelle • Franz Schubert

Le charme • Ernest Chausson

Le secret • Gabriel Fauré

Aurore • Gabriel Fauré

Clair de lune • Gabriel Fauré

El majo discreto • Enrique Granados

En Jerez de la Frontera • Joaquín Rodrigo

Canción de cuna • Xavier Montsalvatge